Islam:  ...g the

Critics

By Zia U. Sheikh, PhD.

FOR DIANNE SOLIS

Ordering Information:

Quantity sales: Special discounts are available on quantity purchases by non-profits, corporations, associations, and others. For details, visit www.silencingthecritics.com.

First Edition, 2012.

Written by Zia U. Sheikh, PhD. (Author)

Foreword by Mehrab Raza of www.quranweekly.com.

Cover photo courtesy of Hannah Hye Photography, copyright protected.

I and the public know what all schoolchildren learn,

Those to whom evil is done

Do evil in return.

Wystan Hugh Auden 1907-1973

About the Author

Zia U. Sheikh was born in Azad Kashmir, and at the age of four he migrated to England with his parents. He has resided in the United States since 1996.

He has memorized the complete Quran. At the age of sixteen, he started an Islamic Theology course, which consisted of Arabic Syntax, Etymology and Grammar, Logic, Quranic Exegesis, Hadith Exegesis, Comparative Religions, Islamic Jurisprudence of the four main schools of thought, Foundations of Jurisprudence, Quran and Hadith, and other subjects. After extensive studying for twelve years, he graduated in 1994 with a Masters in Islamic Theology. He has since completed his PhD thesis with the Graduate Theological Foundation, attaining his doctorate in 2011.

He continues to actively build bridges between faiths by engaging in interfaith dialogue, giving lectures, and presentations on Islam in colleges, universities, and churches throughout the United States.

Content

Foreword

By Mehrab Reza

Following the events of 9/11, my religion was hijacked by multiple organizations. Not only by the religious extremists; religious extremists and fanatics are no longer alone in their efforts to pervert the message of the *Qur'an*, the written word of God. Their ranks have now been bolstered by the news media, literature, politicians, propaganda, and the list is continuously growing.

Due to the misdirection of these interest groups, Islam has been masked with a "Bogey-Man" persona and blamed for any misfortune that befalls us. This has led to the citizen support of the unbefitting invasion of Iraq under the delusion of a nuclear threat, torture cells such as Abu Ghraib and Guantanamo, and hate crimes committed against peace-loving Muslims in America.

The amount of unqualified individuals speaking on behalf of my religion has reached unprecedented proportions. It appears that all one must do to gain wealth and fame, for now, is to ascertain himself as an expert on Islam and then proceed to belligerently defame it. I believe that if one is interested in the truth and a proper understanding, then one must meet with those who possess true knowledge.

If I were to inquire about Christianity or Judaism, I would not turn to CNN or swallow the words of preachers of various faiths. No—I would proceed to my nearest church, synagogue, or university and question those who are authorities on the matter. Indulging our minds to inauthentic information is similar to feeding our stomachs ill-prepared food—it will not sit well and can cause undesirable reactions.

The absence of authentic information, the general confusion about Islam, and the antagonistic efforts of the aforementioned interest groups are the driving forces behind my book. My intentions are not to convert anyone to Islam or bash any religion. My book is a simple explanation of what we Muslims believe our religion to be, and why the attacks made against us are counterfeit. You may go and dig up books dating back 800 years explaining our theology and why we submit ourselves to the will of God. But if you deplore complex reasoning and exhaustive psychoanalysis, then read it here.

Introduction

Since the tragic events of 9/11, Islam and Muslims have been going through many challenges in the West. If it wasn't enough to have their religion hijacked by terrorists, it was re-hijacked by so-called experts on Islam, each "expert" claiming to know more than the other about the "reality" of Islam.

When this happened, a discourse took over the country, particularly from the conservative right, about the "threat" of Islam to American society, freedom, and values. Each and every action or ruling that was laid down by the government or a judge that was in favor of Muslims, reflected, in the view of these self-proclaimed experts, the victory of Islam over these long-established American values.

Subsequently, an industry developed out of this fear of "Islam is taking over," so much so that the fear-mongering reached proportions of hysteria. Anyone who jumped on the bandwagon of scaring people the most about Islam stood to make an infinite amount of money.

More than ten years later, that industry is still going strong. More and more ludicrous claims have been made by this industry against Islam and Muslims, and those claims are eagerly gobbled up by the American public.

Because of the successful campaigns of these Islamophobes, Muslims have had to defend their faith from all kinds of criticisms. We have had to endure barrages of negative media propaganda, and physical attacks on our mosques, our houses, and our families. We have a harder time proving our worth to prospective employers at job interviews. And despite all the condemnation of terrorism that we have proclaimed, we are still asked, "Why don't you condemn terrorism?" or "Why are Muslims silent?", and questions along a similar vein.

Additionally, the right-wing echo chamber unifies on anti-Islamic talking points and further maligns Islam, conveniently hiding the fact that the majority of Muslims worldwide are peace-loving people who have nothing to do with the extremism that they portray as being exclusively Islamic.

Well I am a Muslim. But I am not a terrorist. I am certainly not a terrorist sympathizer. So why am I writing this book? You will see in the following chapters all the adverse factors that are fueling my frustration, and compelling me to do something to set the record straight. That is why I am writing this book.

I am a proud American Muslim. No, it's not an oxymoron. I am proud of being an American, and I am proud of being a Muslim. And I speak on behalf of all American Muslims who are frustrated and angry like me. I hold a very prominent position amongst American Muslims. I am a community leader, educated, and hold a doctorate in my field of study.

I am sure that after reading this book, certain people will be hell-bent on assassinating my character. Reza Aslan, who is regarded as a liberal by most Muslims, didn't even escape the wrath of the conservative critics when he wrote his book, *No God but God,* so I am sure that I will also become a target of such abuse. The same can be said about the now infamous Imam Faisal Abdul Rauf, regarded as a liberal by Muslims, and accepted amongst all levels of society as "tolerant", until the Ground Zero Mosque fiasco erupted, painting him as a terrorist sympathizer, hell-bent on building his "victory mosque" a few blocks away from the grounds of the terrorist attacks of September 11.

Even if I do become the target of such hatemongers, if I can educate people about Islam, and silence those critics once and for all, it will have been completely worth the sleepless nights and hard work involved in doing the research for this daunting project.

The purpose of this book is once and for all to answer all those criticisms that are directed at Islam, so that we don't have to continuously and repeatedly answer the same questions, criticisms and accusations. Each chapter will have a heading highlighting the point of debate, which will then be discussed in the chapter itself, hopefully in a clear and unambiguous way, so that all criticisms can be countered.

If those anti-Islamic critics and their followers can be educated, and therefore silenced, through the power of the written word, then this book will have fulfilled its purpose.

"Why don't Muslims condemn terrorism?"

This question is the most frequently asked, and it comes in various forms, sometimes as a question, and sometimes as a statement, like, "If only the Muslim majority were not silent, we would trust them more."

It becomes even more painful to see academics, supposedly educated people, presenting the same kind of rhetoric. In an op-ed column in the New York Times, published on July 8, 2005, renowned and otherwise respected journalist Thomas Friedman declared in an article entitled, *If It's a Muslim Problem, It Needs a Muslim Solution* that "The Muslim village has been derelict in condemning the madness of jihadist attacks... To this day - to this day - no major Muslim cleric or religious body has ever issued a fatwa condemning Osama bin Laden."

The reality is that Muslims have been condemning terrorism, individually and through organizations, and even through royal decrees. But the media doesn't pick up on these announcements and condemnations, because it's simply not exciting. It's not newsworthy. And God forbid, the news media organizations wouldn't want people to realize that Muslims are actually peaceful!

All you have to do is a quick search on Google, using the search words "fatwa[1] against terrorism" or "Muslims condemn extremism". You will literally find hundreds of websites that condemn terrorism.

One of the most prominent organizations in the USA, The *Fiqh* Council of North America, has issued the following religious decree:

"The *Fiqh* Council of North America wishes to reaffirm Islam's absolute condemnation of terrorism and religious extremism.

Islam strictly condemns religious extremism and the use of violence against innocent lives. There is no justification in Islam for extremism or terrorism. Targeting civilians life and property through suicide bombings or any other method of attack is *haraam* or forbidden - and those who commit these barbaric acts are criminals, not martyrs.

The *Qur'an*, Islam's revealed text, states:

"Whoever kills a person [unjustly], it is as though he has killed all of mankind. And whoever saves a life, it is as though he had saved all mankind." 2

Prophet Muhammad said there is no excuse for committing unjust acts:

---

[1] Fatwa means a religious ruling or decree issued by an Islamic authority.
[2] The Holy *Qur'an*, Chapter 5, verse 32

"*Do not be people without minds of your own, saying that if others treat you well you will treat them well, and that if they do wrong you will do wrong to them. Instead, accustom yourselves to do good if people do good and not to do wrong (even) if they do evil.*" 3

God mandates moderation in faith and in all aspects of life when He states in the *Qur'an*:

"*We made you to be a community of the middle way, so that (with the example of your lives) you might bear witness to the truth before all mankind*".4

In another verse, God explains our duties as human beings when he says:

"*Let there arise from among you a band of people who invite to righteousness, and enjoin good and forbid evil.*"5
Islam teaches us to act in a caring manner to all of God's creation. The Prophet Muhammad, who is described in the Qur'an as a mercy to the worlds said:

"*All creation is the family of God, and the person most beloved by God (is the one) who is kind and caring toward His family.*"

In the light of the teachings of the *Qur'an* and *Sunnah* we clearly and strongly state:

---

3 Tirmidhi
4 The Holy *Qur'an*, Chapter 2, Verse 143
5 The Holy *Qur'an*, Chapter 3, Verse 104

All acts of terrorism targeting civilians are *haraam* (forbidden) in Islam. It is *haraam* for a Muslim to cooperate with any individual or group that is involved in any act of terrorism or violence.

It is the civic and religious duty of Muslims to cooperate with law enforcement authorities to protect the lives of all civilians.

We issue this fatwa following the guidance of our scripture, the *Qur'an*, and the teachings of our Prophet Muhammad peace be upon him. We urge all people to resolve all conflicts in just and peaceful manners.

We pray for the defeat of extremism and terrorism. We pray for the safety and security of our country, the United States, and its people. We pray for the safety and security of all inhabitants of our planet. We pray that interfaith harmony and cooperation prevail both in the United States and all around the globe."[6]

The above decree is then signed by the members of the *Fiqh* Council of North America, followed by signatures of hundreds of Islamic organizations, mosques, and individuals.

In fact, if you were to visit the website www.theamericanmuslim.org you will find lists of literally hundreds of Islamic religious authorities condemning terrorism.

---

[6]http://theamericanmuslim.org/tam.php/features/articles/*Fiqh*_council_of_north_america_issues_fatwa_against_terrorism/

So the answer to the question posed at the beginning of this chapter can easily be found. You just have to know where to look, and have the willingness to find it.

Now that we have determined that Muslims have in fact condemned terrorism, the question remains; why *should* Muslims condemn terrorism so vocally? The fact that one is not engaging in any crime is proof enough that the person disapproves of that particular action. And we know that the majority of Muslims are law-abiding, peaceful citizens.

Many people are not aware that even after slavery has been abolished for so many years, segregation has been outlawed throughout the United States, and discrimination based on racial background is illegal, the Ku Klux Klan still has a presence throughout the country.

Even in recent years, the Klan has been active in carrying out attacks against black and multicultural families. Here are a few examples:

In April 2003, five members of the American Invisible Empire of the Ku Klux Klan were convicted in federal court in Louisiana on conspiracy and intimidation charges for burning a cross at the house of three African-American men in Longville, Louisiana. The five men, who all pleaded guilty, had burned the cross in an attempt to force the victims into leaving the area. All three victims did move out.

At the sentencing in that case, U.S. District Judge Tucker Melancon expressed the un-American role that the Klan plays in the United States, saying that "while foreign terrorists would kill our bodies and destroy our buildings, the American Invisible Empire and the Ku Klux Klan and what they stand for and the type of conduct these defendants engaged in to rid themselves of their black neighbors, attacks our nation's very soul."

Klan members are also known for engaging in acts of domestic terrorism. In March 2006, for example, six members of the Nation's Knights of the Ku Klux Klan pleaded guilty to a whole host of weapons and conspiracy charges in connection with an illegal gun trading scheme in the early 2000s to finance a plan to blow up the Johnston County, North Carolina, courthouse.

In August 2005, North Georgia White Knights member Daniel James Schertz pleaded guilty to building pipe bombs designed to blow up buses carrying Mexican and Haitian migrant workers from Tennessee to Florida. In November 2005, he received a 170-month federal prison sentence.

In 2003, Pennsylvania Klan leader David Hull was convicted of illegal weapons charges in connection with an alleged plot to use hand grenades to attack abortion clinics; he also allegedly told an informant that he had turned his car into a "suicide bomb on wheels".

In 1997, in one of the more ambitious cases, three Klansmen and a Klanswoman—Edward Taylor, Jr., Shawn Dee Adams, Catherine Dee Adams, and Carl Waskom, Jr.—were arrested for plotting a series of terrorist acts in north Texas, including an attack on a natural gas processing plant. This would serve as a diversion for a $2 million armored car robbery designed to finance further acts of domestic terrorism. While surveying the natural gas refinery, Klan members noticed children nearby and realized they would be likely victims of a blast. "But if it has to be," Catherine Dee Adams said, in words caught on tape, "I hate to be that way, but if it has to be..." However, because another Klan member had reservations and alerted the police, the plot was foiled before it could be carried out. The four were arrested in April 1997 and eventually pleaded guilty to a variety of charges.[7]

In all of the above scenarios, is it feasible to demand an apology from every single white American based upon the actions of the corrupt few, as exemplified in the above cases. It is quite obvious that we do not demand an apology or condemnation from everyone just because of a few bad apples.

Similarly, is it reasonable for any non-Hispanic person to demand all "Hispanic people" condemn the drug trade? Even though we are fully cognizant of the fact that the majority of

---

[7]http://www.adl.org/learn/ext_us/kkk/crime.asp?LEARN_Cat=Extremi sm&LEARN_SubCat=Extremism_in_America&xpicked=4&item=kkk with some editing.

drugs smuggled into the United States are coming from Hispanic countries, nobody demands that Hispanics make such a declaration.

So why should Muslims have to be coerced, even implicitly, into making such declarations against terrorism, when the majority of Muslims have nothing whatsoever to do with active terrorism?

The Islamophobes, and their *Modus Operandi*

There is a group of individuals that work in tandem with each other to magnify the perceived threat of Islam and Muslims. Let's use an appropriate name for such people. A reasonable label might be "Islamophobe", which I will use throughout this book.

The way that the Islamophobes work is as follows:

Right-wing neo-conservative authors take one talking point and start repeating it over and over again. The right-wing media--such as Fox News--and right-wing websites--such as WorldNetDaily and Frontpagemag--then broadcast and loop the same message in a perpetual echo-chamber. Finally, right-wing politicians jump on board and begin repeating the same message to instill mass hysteria in the general public. Conceive an invalid point, reiterate exhaustively, accomplish hysteria, paranoia, and panic; this is the pattern that one can clearly see.

Examples of such echo-chamber talking points are phrases such as "Creeping *Shariah*", or "Stealth Jihad". These have become commonly used phrases to denote the perceived threat of Islam taking over the USA.

If you pay particular attention, you will notice all of the people involved in producing this mass hysteria are actually interconnected, and work together for a common goal, namely to undermine the religion of Islam.

It is true that people who make any kind of future plan usually do so by taking note of previous successful campaigns. During the Second World War, the United States Office of Strategic Services described Adolf Hitler's psychological profile:

"His primary rules were: never allow the public to cool off; never admit a fault or wrong; never concede that there may be some good in your enemy; never leave room for alternatives; never accept blame; concentrate on one enemy at a time and blame him for everything that goes wrong; people will believe a big lie sooner than a little one; and if you repeat it frequently enough people will believe it sooner or later."

Is there any difference between the methodology adopted by Hitler to undermine the Jews and today's Islamophobes who attempt to malign Islam and Muslims? Intelligent people will see that both groups' methods are not dissimilar.

Most of the Islamophobes have been exposed by a website called loonwatch.com, which details the way that they work, and exposes mistakes that they have made in their criticism of Islam. I strongly suggest that the readers of this book to visit this website.

The following individuals are names of Islamophobes that you may come across:

1. Pamela Geller
2. David Horowitz
3. Daniel Pipes
4. Robert Spencer
5. Steve Emerson
6. Brigitte Gabriel
7. Walid Shoebat
8. Kamal Saleem
9. Zachariah Anani
10. Frank Gaffney
11. Ayaan Ali Hirsi
12. Geert Wilders

Some of the above individuals have been mentioned in a detailed and well-researched report entitled *Fear Inc: The Roots of the Islamophobia Network in America* by the Center for American Progress.[8] I encourage everyone to download and read this report.

I will also give you a little background on these individuals, so that you can become aware of whom these people really are, and the nefarious methods and talking points that they employ.

Pamela Geller

According to her own website, Pamela Geller is the founder, editor and publisher of AtlasShrugs.com and executive director

---

[8]http://www.americanprogress.org/issues/2011/08/pdf/islamophobia.pdf

of the American Freedom Defense Initiative (AFDI) and Stop Islamization of America (SIOA) in partnership with Robert Spencer. She is the author of *Stop the Islamization of America: A Practical Guide to the Resistance* and *The Post-American Presidency: The Obama Administration's War on America* with Robert Spencer. She is also a regular columnist for *World Net Daily*, Andrew Breitbart's *Big Government and Big Journalism*, the *American Thinker*, and other publications.

The name of her website is a play of a novel by Ayn Rand, *Atlas Shrugged,* in which the author talks about the philosophy of not promoting the welfare state, and promoting individualism, capitalism, objectivism, and above all rational egoism, the principle that an action is rational if and only if it maximizes one's self-interest. This basically highlights the philosophy of the current Republican Party, which looks after the interests of the rich and industrious, and downplays the importance of the social needs of the working class and poor.

She was mentioned as an inspiration by the Norwegian terrorist, Anders Behring Breivik, a Christian right-wing extremist who confessed to a bombing and mass shooting that killed 77 people on July 22, 2011, with the excuse of "protecting Norwegian society from Muslims". She subsequently defended the attack, accusing the victims to be part of "anti-Israeli indoctrination", and that participants in the camp were "future leaders of the party responsible for flooding Norway with Muslims who refuse to assimilate, who commit major violence against Norwegian natives including violent gang rapes, with impunity, and who live on the dole."[9]

She is also mentioned as a key player in the detailed report entitled *Right Wing Playbook on Anti-Muslim Extremism*[10] by People for the American Way website.

Her application to trademark her movement *Stop the Islamization of America* was refused by the government because of its anti-Islamic nature.

She was one of the main critics of the so-called Ground Zero mosque, mobilizing thousands of people around the country to fight against the building of a cultural center, not a mosque that was not even at Ground Zero. This mobilization led to protests against many proposed mosques around the country, even in far-off locations such as Murfreesboro, Tennessee.

She is notorious for making unfounded and baseless claims, such as:

1. President Obama is the secret lovechild of Malcolm X
2. President Obama was not born in the United States
3. Nazis adopted the Muslim Idea of Jihad
4. All Muslim Chaplains are Jihadists
5. Muslims engage in Bestiality

---

[9] http://thinkprogress.org/security/2011/08/01/284011/pam-geller-race-mixing-breivik-right/?mobile=nc
[10] http://www.pfaw.org/rww-in-focus/the-right-wing-playbook-anti-muslim-extremism

6. Calling for the nuking of Mecca, Madinah, and Tehran
7. Calling for the destruction of the Golden Dome in Jerusalem

In addition, she is another "Stealth Jihad" conspiracy theorist, and some of her weirdest and wackiest statements will be discussed later.

David Horowitz

David Horowitz is responsible for the introduction of "Islamofascism" week in universities and colleges across the United States. The purpose behind this controversial endeavor is to portray Islam and Muslims in a bad light by emphasizing that Islam is equated with fascist ideals.

Horowitz himself has a very checkered past. Online searches show him to have a Marxist Communist upbringing. He rejected, according to his claims, those ideals and adopted a conservative attitude later in life, writing books on the subject.

According to his filed tax returns, Horowitz, through his David Horowitz Freedom Center, funds the website Jihadwatch, which will be discussed later.

Some of the controversies surrounding Horowitz include:

1. On the Riz Khan show, on Al-Jazeera television, televised on August 21st, 2008, Horowitz claimed that

the Prophet Muhammad called for the *"extermination of Jews"*.

2. On the same show, Horowitz also stated that he supports the *"creation of a Palestinian State in Jordan"* in complete opposition to international law's "two-state" model.

3. Online searches expose him in many videos using Anti-Muslim, Anti-Palestinian and pro-Zionist rhetoric.

His passion for the neo-conservative agenda has made him a celebrity amongst the right wing, to such an extent that even awards are named after him.

Daniel Pipes

Unlike other Islamophobes listed, Pipes actually has an academic background in the study of Islam. He attained a doctorate from Harvard, writing a thesis on Medieval Islamic History. He also spent time in Cairo, studying Arabic and the Qur'an.

Despite having studied Islam so deeply, he harbors grave misunderstandings about the Islamic religion. In an op-ed piece in the Dallas Fort Worth Star Telegram dated December 30, 2004, he stoked controversy by approving of Japanese-style internment camps for Muslims.

"For years, it has been my position that the threat of radical Islam implies an imperative to focus security measures on Muslims. If

searching for rapists, one looks only at the male population. Similarly, if searching for Islamists (adherents of radical Islam), one looks at the Muslim population. And so, I was encouraged by a just-released Cornell University opinion survey that finds nearly half the U.S. population agreeing with this proposition. Specifically, 44 percent of Americans believe that government authorities should direct special attention toward Muslims living in the United States, either by registering their whereabouts, profiling them, monitoring their mosques or infiltrating their organizations. That's the good news; the bad news is the near-universal disapproval of this realism. Leftist and Islamist organizations have so successfully influenced public opinion that polite society shies away from endorsing a focus on Muslims. In the United States, this intimidation results in large part from a revisionist interpretation of the evacuation, relocation and internment of ethnic Japanese during World War II."

Pipes is one of the founders of *Campuswatch,* an organization dedicated to promote the state of Israel and undermine the state of Palestine in college campuses nationwide, although the stated aim is to promote academic freedom and dissent towards academics who force their own academic opinions onto students.

Other controversial statements and actions attributed to Pipes include:

1. In the National Review on January 19th 2010, he wrote a column entitled *Why I stand with Geert Wilders,* stating

that the controversial, outspoken right-wing Dutch politician "is the most important European alive today" ..."Because he is best placed to deal with the Islamic challenge facing the continent. He has the potential to emerge as a world-historical figure."

2. In 1990, Pipes wrote an article in the National Review, stating, "Western European societies are unprepared for the massive immigration of brown-skinned peoples cooking strange foods and maintaining different standards of hygiene ... All immigrants bring exotic customs and attitudes, but Muslim customs are more troublesome than most."

3. On his own website and in articles for *The Jerusalem Post*, Pipes claimed that Barack Obama was a former Muslim.[11] He alleged that Obama falsely claims that he had never been a Muslim, and that "the campaign appears to be either ignorant or fabricating when it states that Obama never prayed in a mosque."[12]

4. Pipes wrote an article for *FrontPage Magazine* entitled "Confirmed: Barack Obama Practiced Islam." According to Pipes, "this matters" because Democratic presidential candidate Obama "is now what Islamic law calls a *murtadd* (apostate), an ex-Muslim converted to another religion who must be executed", and as

---

[11] The Jerusalem Post, August 25 2008
[12] Danielpipes.org December 24, 2007 with subsequent additions

president this would have "large potential implications for his relationship with the Muslim world.[13]

5. In 1987, Pipes encouraged the United States to provide Iraqi dictator Saddam Hussein with weapons and intelligence to combat Iran in the Iran–Iraq War. He wrote that "Iraq has a history of anti-Americanism, anti-Zionism, support for terrorism, and friendliness toward the Soviet Union", but "If our tilt toward Iraq is reciprocated, moreover, it could lay the basis for fruitful relationship in the longer term."[14]

6. In a *National Review* article dated February 2, 2010, Pipes suggested that the way that Barack Obama could save his presidency is by bombing Iran. He states, that President Obama must "give orders for the U.S. military to destroy Iran's nuclear-weapon capacity ... The time to act is now."[15]

These are just some of the controversial statements attributed to Pipes. He remains one of the pioneers of the anti-Islam movement.

Robert Spencer

Robert Spencer is the director of Jihadwatch, an anti-Islamic website, and has authored many books critical of Islam. As one

---

[13] Frontpage Magazine January 7, 2008
[14] Pipes, Daniel; Mylroie, Laurie (April 27, 1987). "Back Iraq: It's time for a U.S. 'tilt'". *The New Republic.*
[15] Pipes, Daniel (February 2, 2010). "How to Save the Obama Presidency: Bomb Iran". *The National Review.*

of his book's title suggests; *Stealth Jihad: How Radical Islam is Subverting America without Guns or Bombs,* Spencer, along with his close friends Pamela Geller and Frank Gaffney, is another Stealth Jihad conspiracy theorist, suggesting that Muslims are taking over American society using sneaky stealth tactics. His books have come under scrutiny for mistakes, omissions, and a biased anti-Islamic approach.

Because of the mistakes that he has made in his books, his credentials have come under scrutiny, especially from the aforementioned loonwatch.com, which insists that his educational background doesn't make him an authority on Islam.

Controversies and criticisms related to Spencer include the following:

1. The Anti-Defamation League condemned Spencer because he "seeks to rouse public fears by consistently vilifying the Islamic faith and asserting the existence of an Islamic conspiracy to destroy 'American' values.[16]
2. In an article in the Financial Times, Karen Armstrong stated that Spencer "cherry-picked" verses of the *Qur'an* to further his agenda. She states, "Spencer never cites the *Qur'an's* condemnation of all warfare as an 'awesome evil', its prohibition of aggression or its

---

[16] http://www.adl.org/main_Extremism/sioa.htm

insistence that only self-defense justifies armed conflict..."[17]

3. Despite being well-known to be quite liberal compared to more conservative Islamic standards, the late Benazir Bhutto accused Spencer of "falsely constructing a divide between Islam and West". She said he was presenting a "skewed, one-sided, and inflammatory story that only helps to sow the seed of civilizational conflict" in his presentation of Islam.[18]

4. Spencer endorsed the English Defense League, a racist right-wing hate group in Britain, saying that "The EDL is standing up to violent thugs from both the Left and the increasingly assertive Islamic communities in Britain, and they deserve the support of all free people."[19]

5. The Southern Poverty Law Center has named Spencer and SIOA co-founder Pamela Geller as the founders of an anti-Muslim hate group. In the Summer 2011 issue of *Intelligence Report*, published by the SPLC, Robert Steinback listed Spencer as a member of the "anti-Muslim inner circle", noting that "Spencer has been

---

[17] Armstrong, Karen (April 27, 2007). "Balancing the Prophet". Financial Times

[18] Benazir Bhutto, Reconciliation: Islam, Democracy, and the West, Harper, 2008, pp. 245-6

[19] Spencer, Robert (March 21, 2010). "UK: Fascist 'anti-fascists' attack anti-jihad demonstrators". Jihad Watch. Retrieved November 1, 2010.

known to fraternize with European racists and neo-fascists."[20]

Because of his passion of promoting his bigoted viewpoints, he is somewhat of a celebrity in anti-Islamic neoconservative circles, and has a huge following.

Steve Emerson

Emerson is a self-proclaimed expert on terrorism, "considered one of the leading authorities on Islamic extremist networks, financing and operations" according to his own website. He is one of the oldest critics of Islam and Muslims, and is vocally pro-Israel and anti-Palestinian. He is the executive director of the *Investigative Project on Terrorism*, whose objective is to be critical of Islam and Muslims, although their stated claim is to be focused on extremism.

He is known for many gaffes in his career, including one that almost led India and Pakistan into a nuclear war![21] Some critics claim that it was done on purpose to promote a public perception that Pakistan was the bad party amongst Asia's nuclear powers, especially since Pakistan has never recognized Israel, and India's nuclear program was reportedly linked to Israel. According to an article in the *Indian Express*, dated June 6th

---

[20] Steinback, Robert (Summer 2011). "The Anti-Muslim Inner Circle". Intelligence Report, Issue #142. Southern Poverty Law Center. Retrieved June 27 2011.

[21] http://www.fair.org/index.php?page=1443

1998, Pakistani politicians were "convinced that they were about to be attacked by India, possibly with Israeli assistance."

Famous criticisms of Emerson include the following:

1. *The Columbia Journalism Review* noted that passages in Emerson's book, *The Fall of Pan Am 103* bore "a striking resemblance in substance and style" to reports in the *Post-Standard* of Syracuse, N.Y; in other words, he plagiarized the reports.[22] Reporters from the newspaper actually cornered him at a conference and forced an apology out of him.

2. *A New York Times* review dated May 19th 1991 of his book *Terrorist* stated that it was "marred by factual errors...and by a pervasive anti-Arab and anti-Palestinian bias."

3. Reporter Robert Friedman, in an article in *The Nation,* dated May 15, 1995, accused Emerson of "creating mass hysteria against American Arabs."

4. He wrongly accused Yugoslavians of the first World Trade Center bombing, on CNN, on March 2nd 1993.

5. He claimed wrongly that the TWA 800 had been brought down by a bomb, on CNBC, on a program aired on August 23rd 1996.

6. As a consultant on a 1997 series on American Muslims by the Associated Press, Emerson presented what he

---

[22] Gloria Cooper (July 1990). "Darts and Laurels". Columbia Journalism Review

claimed were FBI documents describing mainstream Muslims with alleged terrorist sympathies. In fact, all the papers were actually his own, and he had deleted all references on the papers that could trace the information back to him. This was uncovered when a reporter found an identical, unedited version by him. Subsequently, all information that Emerson had provided was removed from the series.

7. Emerson's most notorious gaffe was his claim that the 1995 Oklahoma City bombing showed "a Middle Eastern trait" because it "was done with the intent to inflict as many casualties as possible."[23]

8. According to a March 1995 article in *Jewish Weekly*, Emerson states. "The level of vitriol against Jews and Christianity within contemporary Islam, unfortunately, is something that we are not totally cognizant of, or that we don't want to accept. We don't want to accept it because to do so would be to acknowledge that one of the world's great religions -- which has more than 1.4 billion adherents -- somehow sanctions genocide, planned genocide, as part of its religious doctrine."

9. Alexander Cockburn states in an article that, "Mr. Emerson's prime role is to whitewash Israeli governments and revile their critics."[24]

---

[23] CBS News, April 19, 1995
[24] Alexander Cockburn, *Wall Street Journal,* June 14th, 1990

10. Jane Hunter states, "There are thousands of ax-grinders in journalism, pushing tantalizing stories with few verifiable facts. Most collect rejection slips, but Steven Emerson finds one respectable media outlet after another for his work, which is sometimes nimble in its treatment of facts, often credulous of intelligence sources, and almost invariably supportive of the Israeli government."[25]

Despite all of the negativity surrounding Emerson, he continues to be summoned to talk shows and interviews for his "expert opinions" on terrorism.

Brigitte Gabriel

She was born in 1964, and claims to have lived for seven years in a bomb shelter during the Lebanese wars, surviving on stale water and grass. She writes "doom and gloom" books, warning people that the Islamic takeover of America is imminent, and when that happens, we will all lose our democratic freedoms. The *New York Times Magazine* described Brigitte Gabriel as a "radical Islamophobe."

She blames her seven years in a bomb shelter on Islamic extremists. Critics of her claims include Lebanese locals who lived in the area at that time. They say that it was impossible for anyone to live in a bomb shelter for seven years, as the fighting happened for a few days at a time, and then there was

---

[25] Jane Hunter, *EXTRA*. October/November 1992

a lull and a return to normalcy, then fighting after that. As for surviving on water and grass, the Lebanese say that food was available for purchase even during the fighting.

As for her claim related to Islamic extremists causing the war and forcing her to stay in a bomb shelter, critics say that the period of fighting in which she was growing up, between 1975 and 1982 was between Arab leftists and nationalists, and groups like *Al-Qaeda* and *Hezbollah* had not yet been formed. *Hezbollah* was founded in 1982, and *Al-Qaeda* in 1988.

Although she claims to separate moderate Islam from radical Islam, her books *They Must Be Stopped* and *Because They Hate*, generalizes all Muslims under the word "They". Her talks are also directed at all Muslims in general, not distinguishing between moderate and radical.

The *New York Times* highlights the double-speak that is part of her anti-Islamic repertoire:

"She insists that she is singling out only "radical Islam" or Muslim "extremists" — not the vast majority of Muslims or their faith. And yet, in her speeches and her two books, she leaves the opposite impression. She puts it most simply in the 2008 introduction to her first book, "Because They Hate: A Survivor of Islamic Terror Warns America."

"In the Muslim world, extreme is mainstream," she wrote. She said that there is a "cancer" infecting the world, and said: "The cancer is called Islamofacism. This ideology is coming out of one source: The Koran."[26]

A famous quote of hers also highlights her attitude:

"The difference, my friends, between Israel and the Arab world is the difference between civilization and barbarism. It's the difference between good and evil ... this is what we're witnessing in the Arabic world, they have no soul! They are dead set on killing and destruction. And in the name of something they call "Allah" which is very different from the God we believe ... because our God is the God of love."[27]

A key component of her anti-Islamic presentation, one that she nearly always uses, is as follows:

"America has been infiltrated on all levels by radicals who wish to harm America. They have infiltrated us at the C.I.A., at the F.B.I., at the Pentagon, at the State Department. They are being radicalized in radical mosques in our cities and communities within the United States." When pressed for details about the names of the people that are actually infiltrating, she has a hard time providing names.

Despite her controversies, she has become a key player of the neo-conservative movement because of her claim that she has

---

[26]http://www.nytimes.com/2011/03/08/us/08gabriel.html?_r=1&pagewanted=all
[27] Christians United For Israel annual conference 2007

"been there, done that" and because she claims that she has experienced radical Islam firsthand, and that she understands the *Qur'an* in its original language, Arabic.

Walid Shoebat, Kamal Saleem, Zachariah Anani

They are mentioned together because they all claim to be former terrorists who converted to Christianity. Because of their claim that they were former terrorists, their stories are readily accepted as valid and true, subsequently resulting in many lucrative money-making opportunities by selling books, making speeches and by making personal appearances.

They all make the same kind of outrageous and unfounded claims. There are many discrepancies in their stories. The lack of corroboration in their stories has been pointed out in an article by *The Jerusalem Post* and other publications.[28]

1. Shoebat claims to have worked for the PLO, even planting bombs for them. However, the place that he claims was the bomb site, Bank Leumi in Bethlehem, has no record of a bomb ever exploding at their branch. He could not recall the year that he had planted the bomb, but when pressed, he settled on 1977. His uncle and aunt denied that there had been an attack on any bank.

---

[28] http://www.jpost.com/Features/Article.aspx?id=96502 The Palestinian "terrorist" turned Zionist

2. He claims that is name is an assumed name, because if he used his real name he would be caught, as he has had a $10 million price for his head. However, his family in Palestine was easily found using his "assumed" name.

3. He says that he was indoctrinated as a child "to believe that the fires of hell were an ever-present reality. We were all terrified of burning in hell when we die ... The teachers told us that the only way we could certainly avoid that fate was to die in a martyrdom operation - to die for Islam." However his relatives say that he had an ideologically mild upbringing, and religion did not play a dominant role.

4. Shoebat stated that, "Islam is not the religion of God – Islam is the devil."

5. At other times, as reported by the San Francisco Chronicle, he has stated that Islam is a "Satanic Cult."

6. At a college speech in Milwaukee, he told a group of 1,000 mostly Midwestern students that "Palestinians keep Jewish testicles and breasts in jars".

7. A *New York Times* report[29] on an event that was held at an Air Force Academy event, headlined "Speakers at Academy Said to Make False Claims," stated that "Academic professors and others who have heard the three men speak in the United States and Canada said

---

[29] http://www.nytimes.com/2008/02/07/us/07muslim.html?ref=us Speakers at Academy make False Claims

some of their stories border on the fantastic", the three men in question being Walid Shoebat, Kamal Saleem and Zachariah Anani.

8. Kamal Saleem claims to be descended from a fabricated person with a grandiose name, "The Grand Wazir of Islam". Prof. Douglas Howard, who teaches the history of the modern Middle East at Calvin College in Grand Rapids, Mich., after hearing Mr. Saleem speak at the college, described this claim as "a nonsensical term", as there is no Pope-like hierarchy in Islam. This claim has since been removed from Saleem's website.

9. Kamal Saleem claims that as a child, he infiltrated Israel to plant bombs via a network of tunnels underneath the Golan Heights. Academics interviewed by *New York Times* said that no such incidents have ever been reported.

10. Saleem's website claims that he worked for almost every dictator in the Middle East. "Like a star U.S. college football running back, Kamal ran important terror operations as a young man in the service of Yasser Arafat, under the coaching Abu Yusuf and Abu Zayed (PLO/Fatah). He has worked for, and dined with, Muhamar Kaddafi (dictator of Libya). He has "carried the ball" for Baath Party leaders and military attaches of Saddam Hussein (dictator of Iraq) and Hafez al Assad (dictator of Syria), for Saudi Arabian sheikhs and princes, and for Abdul Rahman (Muslim Brotherhood).

Kamal Saleem fought with the Afghan Mujahedeen for victory against the Soviets ... before he and his patrons turned their attention to the destruction of the West – and Western freedoms – through Islamicization. Above all, Kamal thirsted for jihadic death to America."[30] Any person with an iota of intelligence will tell you that these kinds of claims are ludicrous and bordering on the insane. Most people regard Saleem as an opportunist just like his friend Walid Shoebat.

11. In a critique of Saleem's book, *Blood of Lambs,* the aforementioned Professor Doug Howard offers the following stinging rebuke:

"In *The Blood of Lambs*, Kamal Saleem writes, "I wanted to be like Bond." In these pages he is Bond, James Bond, in size 6XL. He gets those emphatic rivals, *both* the PLO and the Muslim Brotherhood, to recruit him. He recalls the intricate details of raids he carried out at age seven. Abu Jihad[31] himself teaches him how to use an AK-47. He is shown off by Yasser Arafat as a model warrior. In Libya at age 14 he has Muammar Qaddafi gushing in gratitude. In Iraq, he waves to Saddam Hussein. He only meets one man smarter than himself, an American commander of the mujahidin at al-Qaeda, "the base," in Afghanistan. No major war of liberation in the Arab

---

[30] www.kamalsaleem.com
[31] Palestinian military leader and founder of the secular nationalist party *Fatah* (b.1935-d.1988)

world seems to have gone off without Kamal's expertise. He schmoozes with rich oil sheikhs in the Emirates and Saudi Arabia and makes love to the beautiful daughter of one of them in London. Even if one were disposed to give these entertaining claims the benefit of the doubt, the book's frequent mistakes give the reader pause. The Islamic *umma* does not mean one world government, and it is not "coming." The PLO was a secular organization even though Yasser Arafat prayed and quoted the *Qur'an*."[32]

12. Zachariah Anani has also made similar claims. The most outrageous of them is that he has killed 223 people, one of the victims killed by him for waking him up at 3am for prayers.

13. Tom Quiggin, a Canadian expert on global jihadism and Senior Fellow at the Centre of Excellence for National Security in Singapore has questioned the veracity of Anani's story, saying that Anani's tales of terror and murder just don't jibe with the time and place he claims to have been killing. Quiggin says, "It appears to be that Mr. Anani is nothing more than an extremist who is trying to create an imaginative history from a contemporary set of fears and stories". Quiggin also mentioned that "Mr. Anani's myths that he has built up

[32]http://www.booksandculture.com/articles/2010/mayjun/mixed message.html Mixed Message; *The testimony of a self-described former terrorist*

around himself lack validity on a number of key points."

14. Anani has said he's 49 years old, which would mean he was born in 1957 or 1958, said Quiggin. If he joined his first militant group when he was 13, it would have been in 1970 or 1971. But the fighting in Lebanon did not begin in earnest until 1975,

15. Quiggin said, "His story of having made kills shortly after he joined and having made 223 kills overall is preposterous, given the lack of fighting during most of the time period he claims to have been a fighter," Quiggin said. "He also states he left Lebanon to go to Al-Azhar University at the age of 18, which would mean he went to Egypt in 1976. In other words, according to himself, he left Lebanon within a year of when the fighting actually started."[33]

16. Anani has also claimed that his house and car were set on fire in Canada because of his beliefs, but the local police have denied any reports of that happening.[34]

17. Anani has claimed that he survived a beheading attempt, but Quiggin says, "This was not a common practice in Lebanon at any time and again it appears as

---

[33] http://www2.canada.com/components/print.aspx?id=4a479502-4490-408e-bdb5-f2638619a62c
[34] http://www.canada.com/windsorstar/news/story.html?id=4a479502-4490-408e-bdb5-f2638619a62c

though he is attempting to build up his past mythology by playing on current Iraqi-based fears."[35]

18. Anani's bio states he lectured at Princeton University. Cass Cliatt, Princeton's media relations manager, said that never happened. She said Anani was scheduled to lecture there in late 2005 with the Walid Shoebat Foundation, but the event was cancelled and the foundation held a news conference at a nearby hotel.

The most astonishing thing that has been pointed out about the above three individuals is that none of them have been prosecuted for admitting to, in some cases, hundreds of murders. They have easily been able to secure citizenship in their adopted countries, which would have been impossible if there had been actual ties to radical groups, unless they lied on their applications, which would be a crime subjecting them to deportation.

Frank Gaffney

Another one of the "experts" that are frequently called onto Fox News, Gaffney is the founder and president of the American Center for Security Policy.

Frank Gaffney is another "stealth jihad" conspiracy theorist. His claim is that Muslims are on the verge of taking over the country using "stealth jihad" tactics. However, he was

---

[35] http://www.canada.com/windsorstar/news/story.html?id=4a479502
-4490-408e-bdb5-f2638619a62c

embarrassed on live television in an interview on Anderson Cooper 360, after Professor Akbar Ahmad presented hard numbers and simple logic to counter his conspiracy theory claims.[36] The transcript of that interview is in the chapter entitled *Logic Versus Hype in the Shariah Debate.*

The following controversies are linked with Gaffney:

1. Anders Breivik, the Christian Norwegian terrorist that killed 77 people in a bomb and gun rampage listed Gaffney's organization as an inspiration seven times in his 1500 page anti-Islamic manifesto.
2. Gaffney was called to the stand as "an expert on Islamic law" in the court case against the building of the mosque in Murfreesboro, Tennessee. He warned the court of the impending threat of *Shariah* Law upon the nation.
3. Gaffney was one of the main people behind the report *Shariah: The Threat to America,* which emphasizes the threat of Islam to the United States. I will write about this and other so-called "academic reports" later in this book.
4. In February 2010, Gaffney claimed that the Missile Defense Agency's logo looked mysteriously like an Islamic crescent, bolstering his claims that the Obama

administration had been infiltrated by Muslims.[37] The Missile Defense Agency responded to this accusation as "ridiculous", as the logo had been made one year before the 2008 elections – before President Obama took office.

5. In the same article, Gaffney claimed that Team Obama's anti-missile initiatives "seem to fit an increasingly obvious and worrying pattern of official U.S. submission to Islam and the theo-political-legal program the latter's authorities call *Shariah*".

6. In the Ground Zero mosque debacle, Gaffney was at the forefront of accusing the organization that was building the community center of turning Ground Zero into "A Shrine to *Shariah*".[38]

Needless to say, Gaffney is highly revered amongst the anti-Islamic establishment, and continues to try to rile up people against Muslims.

Ayaan Ali Hirsi

She was born in Somalia in 1969, and has become an outspoken critic of Islam and Muslims. She credits this to an upbringing in which, according to her claims, she was the victim of genital mutilation and attempted forced marriage. I will discuss genital mutilation later.

---

[37] http://biggovernment.com/fgaffney/2010/02/24/can-this-possibly-be-true-new-obama-missile-defense-logo-includes-a-crescent/
[38] http://www.familysecuritymatters.org/publications/id.6609/pub_detail.asp

She is the author of *Infidel* and *Nomad,* both books are autobiographical and both are extremely critical of Islam. Although her traumatic experiences that are recounted in the books are deserving of sympathy, they are in no way a reflection of what happens to every single Muslim female, but unfortunately this is how she portrays it, turning her unfortunate experiences into a lifelong vendetta against Islam and Muslims.

Upon review of her book *Nomad*, Nicholas D. Kristof, co-author of *Half the Sky: Turning Oppression Into Opportunity for Women Worldwide,* said that propensity to violence and religious vocabulary and tradition went overboard in her book.

He says, "The third problem is a propensity to violence in the family, as well as in religious vocabulary and tradition," and then, quoting text from her book, he goes on, "I don't want to create the impression that all people from Muslim countries or tribal societies are aggressive," she writes — and then she proceeds to do just that. She declares: "Islam is not just a belief; it is a way of life, a violent way of life. Islam is imbued with violence, and it encourages violence. Muslim children all over the world are taught the way I was: taught with violence, taught to perpetuate violence, taught to wish for violence against the infidel, the Jew, the American Satan."

Kristof continues, "This is the kind of exaggeration that undermines the book. If the points about women and money are largely true, the point about violence seems to me vastly overstated. Yes, corporal punishment is common in madrassas, as it was in the rural Oregon schools where I grew up, and as it continues to be in Texas. Beatings may be regrettable, but they don't typically turn children into terrorists."

At the end of the review, he says, "It's true that public discussion in some Muslim countries has taken on a strident tone, full of over-the-top exaggerations about the West. Educated Muslims should speak out more against such rhetoric. In the same way, here in the West, we should try to have a conversation about Islam and its genuine problems — while speaking out against over-the-top exaggerations about the East. This memoir, while engaging and insightful in many places, exemplifies precisely the kind of rhetoric that is overheated and overstated."[39]

Ian Buruma, who is the Henry Luce professor at Bard College, is the author of the book *Murder in Amsterdam.*

He has written a detailed review in the New York Times for Hirsi's book *Infidel.* His conclusion about the book is similar to that written by Nicolas Kristof mentioned above. He says, "Comparing the lack of aggression in a Dutch school with her own childhood experiences, she concludes that "this is why Somalia is having a civil war and Holland isn't. All this warms

---

[39] http://www.nytimes.com/2010/05/30/books/review/Kristof-t.html?pagewanted=all

the cockles of my Dutch heart, of course, but it offers up the West as a caricature of sweetness and light, which is then contrasted not to specific places, like Somalia, Kenya or Saudi Arabia, but to the whole Muslim world. Because of this, Hirsi Ali tends to fly into a rage when the inhabitants of this Garden of Eden fail sufficiently to appreciate their good fortune. Europeans who argue, for example, that Muslims might feel more at home in the West if we offered a modicum of respect for their religion, instead of insulting them at every turn, are "stupid" or worse, for it is indeed Hirsi Ali's holy mission to "wake these people up," to convince us that the justification for 9/11 was "the core of Islam," and the "inhuman act of those 19 hijackers" is its "logical outcome.

There is no doubt that many Islamic societies, especially in the Middle East, are in deep trouble for many reasons: political, historical, social, economic and religious. Revolutionary Islamism is seen by a growing number of Muslims as the only answer to failed secular dictatorships and corrupt, oil-rich elites, as well as to the economic and military domination of the United States. And European Muslims, often confused and alienated, feel Europe's fatal attraction. Hirsi Ali is quite right that this force must be resisted. Enlightened reform of religious practices that clash with liberal democratic freedoms is necessary. But much though I respect her courage, I'm not convinced that Ayaan Hirsi Ali's absolutist view of a perfectly enlightened West at war with the demonic world of Islam offers the best perspective from which to get this done."[40]

The above two reviews of her books, by educated and well-read and well-traveled non-Muslims, basically sums up the problem with Hirsi. She bundles all Muslims into one monolithic group, not clarifying to her mostly oblivious audience all the different nuances, socio-economic and otherwise, involved in all the diverse Muslim populations of the world. People who are taken in by her rhetoric actually take her seriously, and she is regularly invited to news programs and university campuses to speak.

Geert Wilders

Geert Wilders is a Dutch politician who has become the darling of the American Islamophobes, due to his anti-Muslim stance in the Netherlands.

His outspoken criticism of Islam has gone so far as to demand the banning of the *Qur'an,* controversially comparing it to Adolf Hitler's *Mein Kampf.*

A BBC investigative documentary discovered that a large funding of Wilders' propaganda was undertaken by Zionists in

---

[40]http://www.nytimes.com/2007/03/04/books/review/04buruma.html?pagewanted=2

Israel. These extreme Zionists have an agenda to destroy all of Palestine "by giving the Palestinians a homeland in Jordan".[41]

The same documentary revealed that he had spent his formative years in a *kibbutz* type community in Israel, possibly the reason for his unwavering loyalty to Israel.

Other controversies related to Wilders are as follows:

1. He was also part of the group that was vocal in condemning the building of a mosque near Ground Zero.[42]

2. He made a controversial 17-minute anti-Islamic film entitled *Fitna*, which no Dutch television channel would broadcast due to its bigoted content. Ultimately he was forced to display it online on a website.

3. When he was asked about the possible impact of this movie, he said: "It's not the aim of the movie but people might be offended, I know that. So, what the hell? It's their problem, not my problem."[43]

4. Norway's Christian terrorist, Anders Breivik was also inspired by Wilders' hate speech, mentioning Wilders' PVV party in his hate-filled 1,500 page manifesto,

---

[41] http://www.youtube.com/watch?v=quS1j-sdiaY

[42] http://www.geertwilders.nl/index.php?option=com_content&task=view&id=1712

[43] http://www.bbc.co.uk/news/world-europe-11443211

saying that it was "the only true conservative party" in Europe.

5. Recently, he stood trial in Holland for inciting hate speech against the Muslims, but was acquitted. However, ethnic minorities vowed to take Wilders to a higher court to try to attain justice.

Just like the other Islamophobes mentioned above, Wilders works in cooperation with anti-Islamic, bigoted individuals to attain a goal of undermining Islam and Muslims, and is a frequent visitor to institutions and conferences supporting such causes.

"Muslims worship a Moon-God"

This is one of the most astonishing of the accusations that have ever been made against Islam. The first time I saw this claim was in an evangelical comic-strip type brochure, whose author was a man named Robert Morey. He subsequently wrote a hate-filled book entitled *Islamic Invasion; Confronting the World's fastest Growing Religion*, in which he repeated the claim.

He says:

"During the nineteenth century, Amaud, Halevy and Glaser went to Southern Arabia and dug up thousands of Sabean, Minaean, and Qatabanian inscriptions which were subsequently translated. In the 1940's, the archeologists G. Caton Thompson and Carleton S. Coon made some amazing discoveries in Arabia. During the 1950's, Wendell Phillips, W.F. Albright, Richard Bower and others excavated sites at Qataban, Timna, and Marib (the ancient capital of Sheba)...

The archeological evidence demonstrates that the dominant religion of Arabia was the cult of the Moon-god.

In 1944, G. Caton Thompson revealed in her book, The Tombs and Moon Temple of Hureidha, that she had uncovered a temple of the Moon-god in southern Arabia. The symbols of the crescent moon and no less than twenty-one inscriptions with the name Sin were found in this temple. An idol which may be the Moon-god himself was also discovered. This was later confirmed by other well-known archeologists."[44]

Further "proof" of his ideas is that the Muslims use the crescent symbol on their flags, on the domes and minarets of their mosques. In addition, Muslims follow the lunar calendar.

This accusation of worshipping a moon-god has been refuted by many leading Christian Scholars. Rick Brown, in the *International Journal of Frontier Missions* states:

"Much of the anger expressed in the West has taken the form of demonizing the Islamic religion, to the extent of accusing Muslims of worshipping a demon. A key element of this attack has been the claim of some that the name Allah refers to a demon or at least a pagan deity, notably the so-called "moon god." Such claims have even been made by scholars who are reputable in their own fields but who are poorly acquainted with the Arabic language and Middle-Eastern history. The Kingdom of God, however, is never advanced by being untruthful, so this matter bears further investigation.

---

[44] R. Morey, *The Islamic Invasion: Confronting The World's Fastest-Growing Religion*, 1992, *op. cit.*, pp. 213-215; *idem.*, *The Moon-God God In The Archeology Of The Middle East*, 1994, *op. cit.*, pp. 7-10.

He goes on, *"Those who claim that Allah is a pagan deity, most notably the moon god, often base their claims on the fact that a symbol of the crescent moon adorns the tops of many mosques and is widely used as a symbol of Islam. It is in fact true that before the coming of Islam many "gods" and idols were worshipped in the Middle East, but the name of the moon god was Sîn, not Allah, and he was not particularly popular in Arabia, the birthplace of Islam. The most prominent idol in Mecca was a god called Hubal, and there is no proof that he was a moon god. It is sometimes claimed that there is a temple to the moon god at Hazor in Palestine. This is based on a representation there of a supplicant wearing a crescent-like pendant. It is not clear, however, that the pendant symbolizes a moon god, and in any case this is not an Arab religious site but an ancient Canaanite site, which was destroyed by Joshua in about 1250 BC. There is also an ancient temple in the ruins of the kingdom of Sheba (Saba), in Yemen, and it includes inscriptions to the kingdom's patron god Almaqah. It has been claimed that Almaqah was a moon god, but there is no solid evidence for this, and scholars now think Almaqah was a sun god. If the ancient Arabs worshipped hundreds of idols, then no doubt the moon god Sîn was included, for even the Hebrews were prone to worship the sun and the moon and the stars, but there is no clear evidence that moon-worship was prominent among the Arabs in any way or that the crescent was used as the symbol of a moon god, and Allah was certainly not the moon god's name."*[45]

---

[45] R. Brown, "Who Is "God"?", *International Journal Of Frontier Missions*,

In fact, if Robert Morey had bothered to do some research he would have found the following:

1. The Word *Allah* is very similar to the word Jesus would have used to describe God, as God in Aramaic, the language Jesus spoke, is pronounced *Aalah* or *Aaloh*.[46]

2. Arab Christians use the exact same word *Allah* in their Arabic-language bibles to describe God, and the same thing is used in their conversations.

3. The crescent has no religious significance whatsoever in Islam. It is simply an icon adopted to denote Islam, maybe because the Ottoman Empire , that was based out of Turkey had a crescent flag as a symbol.

4. The lunar calendar is not only followed by Muslims, but also Orthodox Jews.

5. The *Qur'an* addresses Jews and Christians, and tells them that we worship the same God. "And argue not with the People of the Scripture unless it be in (a way) that is better, save with such of them as do wrong; and say: We believe in that which hath been

2006, Volume 23, No. 2, p. 79.
[46] http://www.peshitta.org/cgi-bin/lexicon.cgi

revealed unto us and revealed unto you; our God and your God is One, and unto Him we surrender."[47]

To summarize, *Allah* is actually a linguistic expression for God in Arabic, just like you would say *"Dieu"* in French, *"Gott"* in German, *"Dios"* in Spanish, *"Khuda"* in Farsi, you use the word *Allah* in Arabic.

However, go to any Islam-hating website, and you will find that this baseless accusation is still very popular. Only educating people about what Muslims truly believe will suppress this and other fallacies.

---

[47] The Holy *Qur'an*, Pickthall translation. Chapter 29 (The Spider): verse 46.

"Europe and America are constantly under the threat of Islamic Terrorism"

Since the tragic events of September 11th, 2001, the perceived threat of Islamic terrorism has been trumpeted from every media source, especially the right-wing neo-conservatives mentioned earlier.

However the reality is completely different. The following sections will highlight the reality.

Terrorism in the United States

According to official FBI reports, the threat of Islamic terrorism in minimal compared to other threats, like right-wing neo-Nazi groups, and the Ku Klux Klan. The following statistics were reported by the FBI in their annual report.[48]

---

[48] www.fbi.gov

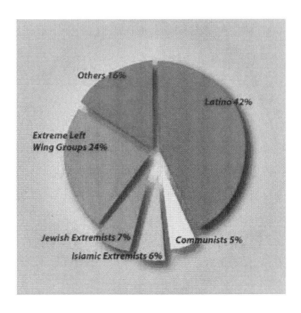

Simply looking at the numbers, we can see that from all forms of extremism, Islamic terrorism is the lowest. However, because of the hyperbole that has become so common since September 11, 2001, people assume that every terrorist act that has occurred or will occur in the future is from Islamic extremists. In fact, one of the above mentioned Islamophobes, Pamela Geller clearly mentioned on her website, referring to a conference that was being conducted by them that the whole purpose of the conference was to scare people.

"This year, Atlas does not disappoint. We are ratcheting it up a few notches. Robert Spencer and I are organizing a joint venture to educate, elucidate and **scare the bejeezus outta ya**. It" (Emphasis added).

Terrorism in Europe

The same kind of hype has been exacerbated in Europe. The Islamophobes sarcastically call Europe "Eurabia" because of their perception that it is turning into the Middle East.

But again, if you look at the numbers, you will find that Islamic extremism in Europe is mainly from separatist groups.

The next few pages present three charts that are published on the Europol website, displaying terrorist figures for the years 2006, 2007, and 2008.

The 2009 report by Europol concludes on page 9:

"Islamist terrorism is still perceived as being the biggest threat worldwide, despite the fact that the European Union (EU) has only faced one Islamist terrorist attack in 2008. This bomb attack took place in the UK. Separatist terrorism remains the terrorism area which affects the EU the most. This includes Basque separatist terrorism in Spain, and France, and Corsican terrorism in France. Past contacts between Euskadi Ta Askatasuna (ETA) and the Revolutionary Armed Forces of Colombia (FARC) illustrate the fact that also separatist terrorist organizations seek cooperation partners outside the EU on the basis of common interests. In the UK, dissident Irish republican groups, principally the Real Irish Republican Army (RIRA) and the Continuity Irish Republican Army (CIRA), and other paramilitary groups may continue to engage in crime and violence."[49]

Europol has been putting terrorism statistics on their websites, taking data from Austria, Belgium, France, Germany, Greece, Ireland, Italy, Poland, Portugal, Spain and the United Kingdom.

Member State	Islamist	Separatist	Left-Wing	Right-Wing	Other/Not Specified	Total
Austria	0	0	0	0	1	1
Belgium	0	0	0	0	1	1
France	0	283	0	0	11	294
Germany	1	0	10	0	2	13
Greece	0	0	25	0	0	25
Ireland	0	1	0	0	0	1
Italy	0	0	11	0	0	11
Poland	0	0	0	1	0	1
Portugal	0	0	1	0	0	1
Spain	0	136	8	0	1	145
UK	0	4	0	0	1	5
Total	1	424	55	1	17	498

FIGURE 1: Terrorist Attacks in 2006 by Type of Terrorism

In 2006 data, (above) there were a total of 498 terrorist attacks. Of those, 424 from separatist groups, 1 was from a right-wing organization, 55 from left-wing organizations, and only 1 from Islamist groups.

[49]http://www.europol.europa.eu/publications/EU_Terrorism_Situation_and_Trend_Report_TE-SAT/TESAT2009.pdf

Member state	Islamist	Separatist	Left Wing	Right Wing	Single Issue	Not Specified	Total 2007
Austria	0	0	1	0	0	0	1
Denmark	1	0	0	0	0	0	1
France	0	253	0	0	0	14	267
Germany	1	15	4	0	0	0	20
Greece	0	0	2	0	0	0	2
Italy	0	0	6	0	0	3	9
Portugal	0	0	0	1	1	0	2
Spain	0	264	8	0	0	7	279
UK	2	-	-	-	-	-	2
Total	4	532	21	1	1	24	583

Figure 2: Number of failed, foiled and successfully executed attacks in 2007 per member state and affiliation

In 2007 data (above), there were a total of 583 terrorist attacks. Of those, 532 from separatist groups, 1 was from a right-wing organization, 21 from left-wing organizations, and only 4 from Islamist groups.

Member State	Islamist	Separatist	Left Wing	Right Wing	Single Issue	Not Specified	Total 2008
Austria	0	5	0	0	0	1	4
France	0	137	0	0	5	5	147
Greece	0	0	13	0	0	1	14
Ireland (Republic of)	0	2	0	0	0	0	2
Italy	0	0	5	0	0	4	9
Spain	0	253	10	0	0	0	263
UK	-	-	-	-	-	-	74
Total 2008	0	397	28	0	5	11	515

Figure 2: Number of failed, foiled or successful attacks in 2008 per member state and per affiliation[6]

In 2008 data, there were a total of 515 terrorist attacks. Of those, 397 from separatist groups, 0 was from a right-wing organization, 28 from left-wing organizations, and 0 from Islamist groups.

All the following data can be found on the Europol web site.

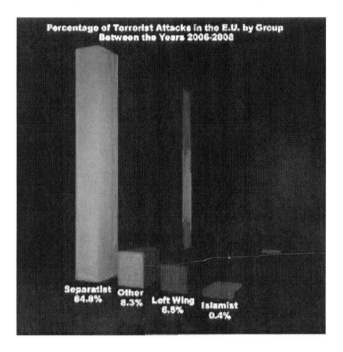

If we sincerely look at the total numbers, we will find that Islamic extremism is the least of Europe's worries. The biggest threat, according to these official statistics, is from separatist groups.

A similar finding has been reported by the Rand Corporation, an influential think tank sponsored by the US government. The report states:

"[Of the] 83 terrorist attacks in the United States between 9/11 and the end of 2009, only three were clearly connected with the jihadist cause. The other jihadist plots were interrupted by authorities."

The Europol report also says:

"The number of [Jihadist] recruits is still tiny. There are more than 3 million Muslims in the United States, and few more than 100 have joined jihad—about one out of every 30,000— suggesting an American Muslim population that remains hostile to jihadist ideology and its exhortations to violence. A mistrust of American Muslims by other Americans seems misplaced...

The homegrown jihadist threat in America today consists of tiny conspiracies, lone gunmen, and one-off attacks...

There is no evidence that America's Muslim community is becoming more radical. Overt expressions of Muslim militancy are muted and rare...

That [overseas] jihadist leaders have been reduced to appeals for others to carry out even small-scale attacks in the United States is evidence of an operational decline that America's homegrown terrorists will not be able to reverse...

That, then, is the threat America faces at home today: tiny conspiracies, lone gunmen, one-off attacks rather than sustained terrorist campaigns (although a lone gunman killing at random could sustain a campaign, as we saw in the case of the Beltway sniper attacks in 2002)."[50]

Yet another report, whose study was funded by a grant from the Department of Justice, notes similar results. The study was conducted by researchers at Duke University and the University of North Carolina at Chapel Hill.[51]

A report by the New York University Center for Human Rights and Global Justice, entitled *Targeted and Entrapped* concludes that the majority of "terrorism" cases that had been prosecuted in the United States were actually cases of entrapment of people who posed no serious threat to the safety of the United States at all.[52] Moreover, the report concludes in great detail that the majority of the indictments took place by relying on the evidence of paid informants, who had a vested interest in justifying the high amounts of money they were receiving by providing "terrorists". A dangerous precedent was created of concentrating on manufactured threats, taking away the focus from truly dangerous people, as was in the case of the Fort Hood massacre.

However many reports we look at, the conclusion is basically the same; that Islamic extremism poses no significant threat to

---

[50]http://www.rand.org/pubs/occasional_papers/2010/RAND_OP292.pdf
[51]http://www.sanford.duke.edu/news/Schanzer_Kurzman_Moosa_Anti-Terror_Lessons.pdf/
[52] http://www.chrgj.org/projects/docs/targetedandentrapped.pdf

the United States or Europe. This doesn't mean that we should become complacent. We should remain vigilant, and report anything suspicious that we encounter, as the general public is usually the first line of defense against any unlawful goings-on.

"*Shariah* Law is taking over the Country"

The modus operandi of the Islamophobes has been mentioned in an earlier chapter. One of the talking points that has been echoed time and again by the same group is that Islamic Law, or *Shariah*, is taking over the country. Phrases used to describe this threat include "Creeping Jihad" and "Stealth Jihad" or "Creeping *Shariah*".

The reason for this accusation is simple. When statistics show that terrorism is not much of a threat to the United States, the Islamophobes have invented a "boogeyman", that cannot be seen or heard, and therefore is a bigger threat than even terrorism. Conveniently, every single Muslim practices *Shariah*, which is deemed a huge threat to the United States; therefore, every single Muslim becomes a potential threat.

This sentiment has even been voiced by most Republican candidates. Newt Gingrich, supposedly one of the more intelligent Republicans, states that "*Shariah* law, is inherently brutal" — defined by oppression, stonings and beheadings. Its triumph is pursued not only by violent jihadists but by stealthy ones attending the mosque down the street. The victory of *Shariah*," he concludes, "would clearly mean the end of the government Lincoln was describing."

This seemingly ominous warning reflects the sentiment of the right-wing, without any proof to back up these threats. The conclusion that one gets from statements such as Gingrich's is that every practicing Muslim is in fact sneakily trying to change the law of the country to make the country based on *Shariah*. Little attention is paid to the fact that 99% of Muslim countries don't even implement *Shariah* law; how could it be implemented in a non-Muslim country?

Gingrich Productions, a production company owned by Newt Gingrich, has even produced a movie, *America at Risk; the War with no Name,* which highlights the same points.[53]

"We should have a federal law that says *Shariah* law cannot be recognized by any court in the United States," Gingrich told the crowd at the conservative Values Voter Summit to a standing ovation. *"The law will let judges know that no judge will remain in office that tried to use Shariah law."*[54]

Herman Cain, a GOP candidate for the 2012 election until allegations of scandalous affairs forced him to step down, also used the word "creeping" in his statement, *"There is this creeping attempt ... to gradually ease Shariah law and the Muslim faith into our government. It does not belong in our government,"* Cain told the liberal blog ThinkProgress.

---

[53] http://www.americaatrisk.com

[54] http://www.politico.com/news/stories/0511/54605_Page2.html

Rick Santorum, another GOP candidate for the 2012 presidential election also stated during a foreign policy speech, "*Shariah* represents an existential threat to America. The enemy is motivated by an interpretation of Islam, *Shariah*, that is antithetical to American civilization."[55]

Sometimes, in their eagerness to portray that "*Shariah* is taking over", and that everything Islamic is inherently evil, the Islamophobes produce some ridiculous notions.

One of the more amusing examples of this was around the time of Thanksgiving in 2011 when the aforementioned Pamela Geller declared on her website that Islam was taking over. Why? Because meat companies that sold Thanksgiving turkeys were now selling *halal* turkeys. She makes the ridiculous claim that eating *halal* meat is tantamount to "losing our freedom". She stated on her website:

"Did you know that the turkey you're going to enjoy on Thanksgiving Day this Thursday is probably halal? If it's a Butterball turkey, then it certainly is – whether you like it or not.

In my book Stop the Islamization of America: A Practical Guide to the Resistance, I report at length on the meat industry's halal scandal: its established practice of not separating halal meat from non-halal meat, and not labeling halal meat as such. And back in October 2010, I reported more little-noted but explosive new revelations: that much of

---

[55] http://www.politico.com/news/stories/0511/54605.html

the meat in Europe and the United States is being processed as halal without the knowledge of the non-Muslim consumers who buy it.

I discovered that only two plants in the U.S. that perform halal slaughter keep the halal meat separated from the non-halal meat, and they only do so because plant managers thought it was right to do so. At other meat-packing plants, animals are slaughtered following halal requirements, but then only a small bit of the meat is actually labeled halal.

Now here is yet more poisonous fruit of that scandal.

A citizen activist and reader of my website AtlasShrugs.com wrote to Butterball, one of the most popular producers of Thanksgiving turkeys in the United States, asking them if their turkeys were halal. Wendy Howze, a Butterball Consumer Response Representative, responded: "Our whole turkeys are certified halal."

In a little-known strike against freedom, yet again, we are being forced into consuming meat slaughtered by means of a barbaric, torturous and inhuman method: Islamic slaughter.

Halal slaughter involves killing the animal by cutting the trachea, the esophagus, and the jugular vein, and letting the blood drain out while saying "Bismillahi-Allahu-akbar"—in the name of God the greatest. Many people refuse to eat it on religious grounds. Many Christians, Hindus or Sikhs and Jews find it offensive to eat meat slaughtered *according to Islamic ritual (although Jews are less likely to be exposed to such meat, because they eat kosher).*

Still others refuse to do so on principle: why should we be forced to conform to Islamic norms? It's Islamic supremacism on the march, yet again.

Non-Muslims in America and Europe don't deserve to have halal turkey forced upon them in this way, without their knowledge or consent. So this Thanksgiving, fight for your freedom. Find a non-halal, non-Butterball turkey to celebrate Thanksgiving this Thursday. And write to Butterball and request, politely but firmly, that they stop selling only halal turkeys, and make non-halal turkeys available to Americans who still value our freedoms."

Although she mentions that Jews are unlikely to consume Halal meat, as they eat kosher, she fails to mention that the method of Islamic slaughter is almost exactly the same as the Jewish method of kosher slaughter. Both methods of slaughter are humane and have been scientifically proven not to hurt the slaughtered animal.

Other wacky claims made by the "Creeping *Shariah*" crowd are as follows:

1. The memorial for Flight 93, which was brought down by terrorists on September 11[th,] is shaped like a crescent, and is facing Mecca.[56]

2. Delta Airlines are encouraging *Shariah* by adding Saudi Arabian Airlines to the Skyteam Alliance.[57]

3. Muslim cabbies stopping to pray on Fridays is a sign that America is becoming subservient to *Shariah*[58]

4. Segregated (male and female segregation) swimming pools in Maryland a sign we are becoming overrun by the Islamic agenda.[59]

5. A manual educating the US army about cultural sensitivities is promoting jihad.[60]

6. Creeping *Shariah* prevents evangelist group from distributing Gospel of John outside an Arab festival in Dearborn, Michigan.[61]

---

[56] http://creepingShariah.wordpress.com/2010/08/29/flight-93-memorial-mosque/

[57] http://www.theblaze.com/stories/is-delta-airlines-showing-signs-of-creeping-*Shariah*-law/

[58] http://atlasshrugs2000.typepad.com/atlas_shrugs/2011/12/takbir-nyc-traffic-snarled-by-muslim-cabbies-stopping-to-pray.html

[59] http://atlasshrugs2000.typepad.com/atlas_shrugs/2011/11/stop-the-islamization-of-america-maryland-public-pools-enforce-*Shariah*-muslim-swim-segregated-swimmin.html

[60] http://atlasshrugs2000.typepad.com/atlas_shrugs/2011/11/us-army-justifies-jihad-about-islam-indoctrinates-soldiers-to-be-culturally-literate-about-islam.html

[61] http://wonkette.com/416253/%E2%80%98creeping-*Shariah*%E2%80%99-leads-to-arrest-of-christians-at-michigan-muslinfest

7. *Shariah* Law "devouring" Great Britain, as Archbishop of Canterbury recommends courts consider *Shariah* to be part of judicial process.[62]

8. Lord Chief Justice Phillips lends support to the idea, by lamenting that there was a "widespread misunderstanding" of *Shariah*.

9. Muslim Arbitration Tribunals puts up a picture of Lord Phillips on their website in appreciation of his endorsement, fueling the hype that Muslims are on the verge of taking over Britain.

10. "To fight home-grown terrorism, Obama to embed Islam in schools"[63], referring to an NPR report[64] that the White House plans to "empower communities by teaching local officials to recognize violent extremism and see the threat as a public safety issue".

11. *Shariah* Opposition becomes litmus test for viability of GOP candidacy according to Politico.com website.[65]

12. Schools teaching (or indoctrinating) students about Islam is a sign of "creeping *Shariah*"[66]. The reality is that the schools were simply teaching students *about* Islam.

---

[62] http://pjmedia.com/blog/*Shariah*-law-already-devouring-uk/?singlepage=true

[63] http://creeping*Shariah*.wordpress.com/2011/12/09/to-fight-homegrown-terrorism-obama-to-embed-islam-in-schools/

[64] http://www.npr.org/2011/12/08/143319965/officials-detail-plans-to-fight-terrorism-at-home

[65] http://www.politico.com/news/stories/0511/54605.html

[66] http://www.jeremiahproject.com/culture/teachingislam.html

All of the above claims by the Islamophobic crowd hint at an impending Muslim takeover of the country. The reality is that there has been no intent on the part of the Muslims to change the constitution whatsoever. Muslims are instructed to abide by the law in whichever country they are living.

As an Imam in the United States, whenever we conduct a marriage ceremony, we always insist that the marriage license from a courthouse is brought to the proceedings; so when the religious ceremony is conducted, the legal requirements are also met, and the Imam signs the legal as well as the religious documentation.

The same thing occurs when the unfortunate incident of divorce takes place. The Imam instructs the divorcing couple to finalize their divorce in an American court, and then bring the divorce decree to the Imam, who finalizes the divorce from a religious perspective.

These examples will give you an insight into how Muslims fulfill their religious obligations, as well as their legal and civil obligations. There are many examples in the same vein.

An independent study has been conducted by the Institute for social policy and understanding (www.ispu.org) which conducted a survey of more than 200 Muslim families, questioning them about their attitudes towards marriage and divorce in American society.

An overwhelming majority of the respondents declared that they had no intention or desire to circumvent the American legal system in conducting their marriages and divorces. A full report can be downloaded from their website.[67]

This attitude of practicing Islam while staying within the system of the American legal framework is the most commonly found attitude amongst American Muslims. You will not find people pushing for *Shariah* law amongst Muslims in the United States.

However, the Constitution of the United States itself allows Muslims and practitioners of all faiths to practice their religion without any fear of persecution.

If we think logically, we will understand that the Constitution of the United States maintains that there should be a clear separation between state and religion. Nobody has been able to circumvent this ruling until now. If anybody could have bridged the gap between religion and state, Christians, the majority of this country, could have done that a long time ago. Yet we see that across federal and state courthouses throughout the United States, there are ongoing disputes about the legal permissibility of publicly displaying religious icons like the Ten Commandments on Federal and State property. So the question is that if the majority population of Christians has

---

[67] http://ispu.org/pdfs/ISPU%20Report_Marriage%20II_Macfarlane_W EB.pdf

not succeeded in amending the constitution to allow something as simple as the display of religious symbols, how is the minority (less than 2%, and according to a Pew poll, 0.8%[68]) of Muslims going to succeed in imposing the whole of *Shariah* law on an uncooperative public? It's worth thinking about!

---

[68] http://people-press.org/files/2011/08/muslim-american-report.pdf

Logic versus Hype in the *Shariah* debate

If anyone makes a claim that *Shariah* law is taking over the country, you should ask them the following questions:

1. What exactly do you mean by "*Shariah* Law is taking over the country"? Can you give examples? The answer that you will get will be a broad statement which will likely make no sense.

2. Who is implementing *Shariah* law? Again, a broad brush will be used to malign all the imaginary Muslims implementing *Shariah* law.

3. Where is *Shariah* law being implemented? There will be no response, because it is not being implemented anywhere.

4. Even in heavily populated Muslims areas, is alcohol, pork and other non-Islamic things available for purchase? The answer is yes, it is available. Then, where is *Shariah* law being implemented?

5. How exactly are Muslims going to implement *Shariah* law in this country, when they are merely 2% (or less) of the population?

6. Does the Constitution of the United States allow religious freedom? If so, why can't Muslims practice

their religion while upholding the law of the land, as they are currently doing?

Unfortunately, when dealing with Muslims, logic seems to go out of the window, and it is replaced by fantasy bordering on hysteria.

A logical approach was undertaken by Dr. Akbar Ahmed in a brief debate televised on CNN, in which the aforementioned Frank Gaffney couldn't respond to clear logical arguments presented by Doctor Ahmed.

Akbar Ahmed, an educated and distinguished academic, is the Ibn Khaldun Chair of Islamic Studies, American University in Washington, D.C., the First Distinguished Chair of Middle East and Islamic Studies at the US Naval Academy, Annapolis, and a Nonresident Senior Fellow at the Brookings Institution.

The following is a transcript of that interview,[69] which highlights the ignorance of people like Gaffney when confronted with an educated academic. The background to this interview is that Gaffney was called as an "expert witness" to testify in a case against the building of a mosque in Murfreesboro, Tennessee, since he jumped on the anti-mosques bandwagon as a result of the Ground Zero mosque controversy.

COOPER: Tonight, new developments in a story we've been following in Murfreesboro, Tennessee, where plans to expand a mosque have

---

[69] http://transcripts.cnn.com/TRANSCRIPTS/1009/27/acd.01.html

created controversy. After the construction plans were approved back in May, protests soon followed.

Now, the Islamic Center of Murfreesboro, which is building the new mosque, has been part of the community for the last 30 years or so without any problems. Last month, though, someone set fire to equipment parked at the construction site. That arson investigation continues. And someone else targeted signs at the site. Now, opponents have filed a lawsuit to block the project. They allege that county officials violated open meeting laws, making the project's approval void. They also argued the planning commission didn't properly vet the backers of the mosque, who they contend may have ties to terrorist sympathizers.

At a hearing today, one witness accused the mosque leaders, including the imam, of being supporters of Shariah law. Now with us is Frank Gaffney, president of Center for Security Policy. He joins me now, along with Akbar Ahmed, the chair of Islamic studies at American University and a former Pakistani ambassador for the United Kingdom. Mr. Gaffney, let me start with you. You testified today in court that there are what you called red flags from a security point of view regarding the mosque. What are those red flags?

FRANK GAFFNEY, PRESIDENT, CENTER FOR SECURITY POLICY: *Well, several were introduced into evidence during the court proceedings. That speak to this issue that you've touched on which is that the imam and others who are involved in the board of the mosque are proponents of Shariah, this totalitarian program, political military* legal program that is absolutely at odds with the Constitution of the United States. In fact, has as its purpose supplanting it. And that kind of seditious activity is, I believe, a red flag that ought to preclude it from being allowed to operate in Murfreesboro or, for that matter, any other community in the United States.

COOPER: But the idea that -- I mean, this is an imam and people have been here for the most part, in this community for many, many years. They've practiced in this community for decades without any problems. And I mean, how are they trying to take over the United States from Murfreesboro, Tennessee?

GAFFNEY: Well, I don't think I suggested that they're trying to take it over from Murfreesboro, Tennessee. I'm suggesting that it's places like Murfreesboro, Tennessee. They are promoting a program that is at odds with our freedoms, our form of government, our Constitution and, to the extent as we've seen in Europe, for example, that this kind of agenda follows the trajectory that it has elsewhere around the world. It ultimately winds up becoming a cancer inside a society. No-go zones are typically associated with it where the authorities dare not go. Shariah law is practiced in those no-go zones. They are expanded in due course. And ultimately, you have the groups like the Muslim Brotherhood, with whom many of these mosques and for that matter, Muslim-American organizations of any note, are associated, pursuing a mission that we know, from evidence introduced into another federal trial, is to destroy western civilization from within. If that's -- that's really worrying.

COOPER: *Ambassador Ahmed, what do you make of what Mr. Gaffney is alleging?*

AHMED: *Well, I think that there is an atmosphere and a cloud of distrust and fear happening over the Muslim community. And I'm concerned about this. In fact, we have visited this particular mosque last year. I went with my team to Columbia in Tennessee, also, where the mosque had been firebombed. So it isn't just an isolated case and that is why I applaud Abe Foxman and the ADF, who have come out with the committee. The committee exclusively to defend and protect mosques throughout the United States of America, and I'm privileged to be a member of that committee.*

COOPER: Do you believe this mosque in Murfreesboro is trying to -- it wants to institute Shariah law in the United States?

AHMED: Anderson, I want you to ask yourself this question, and I'm sure your mathematics is better than mine. If every Muslim in the United States of America, which is about 2 percent of the population, wanted Shariah -- which is not the case at all -- even if they wanted it, could they impose it over a population of 98 percent who are not Muslim in a democracy? In my country where I come from, Pakistan, 98 percent of the population is Muslim. There is no Shariah law. I've been a commissioner in charge of large parts of the country. Our laws are criminal and civil procedure codes derived from British colonial law which go to Westminster, which in turn has influenced the U.S. Constitution. So the notion of Shariah being implemented in America *with about 2 percent of the population, to me, is mathematically absurd.* (Emphasis added)

COOPER: Mr. Gaffney, what about that? I mean...

GAFFNEY: Well, I don't think he answered your question. What is, of course, the case is that today, the numbers of Muslims in America and, indeed, the numbers of Muslims in America that are promoting Shariah are very small, blessedly. This is the time to stop them from trying to move this country in a direction that we dare not have it go. If we in fact...

COOPER: But what evidence do you have that the folks in Murfreesboro are part of this plot linked to the Muslim Brotherhood? I mean, it seems...

GAFFNEY: I -- I've suggested that some of the evidence was introduced in the trial. We have an imam who was trained in al-Azhar (ph.), the central academic institution of Shariah in the world. We have members of the mosque board, who promote Hamas in demonstrations and through their public statements. We have people associated with the mosque who, I think, make no bones about their preference for Shariah. In fact, that is what the authorities of Islam say they are supposed to do.

And this is the problem. Just a second. This is the problem. What Shariah commands is jihad. And in Pakistan as elsewhere, we see that it's taking the form of the violent kind of jihad and, indeed, Shariah law is being encroached into the Pakistani system and, indeed, other systems around the world.

But also, the stealth jihad and this is the real problem with places like this mosque in Murfreesboro. You have stealth jihadists at work, trying to advance the situation.

COOPER: But the FBI investigated.

GAFFNEY: Most of our government is ignoring it.

COOPER: ...apparently, investigated the board member you're talking about there were comments made on his my space page and no charges were brought. Ambassador, just because the imam went to this university in Egypt, should that be a red flag?

AHMED: Of course not, Anderson. This is the oldest university in the Muslim world. It's 1,000 years old. It's expected to teach Islamic jurisprudence. I went to a Catholic school in north Pakistan. Does this mean that I owe allegiance to the pope? That's absurd. Any university in the Muslim world, any university in the Catholic world would teach its own laws, the laws of their particular religion. If this imam has violated the laws of America -- can I please finish? -- if the imam has violated the laws of the land, if he's a threat to the security of the land the authorities should act. But unless we know whether he, in fact, has been promoting -- and I'm not even sure what this concept means: "promoting the Shariah." The Shariah is an abstract. It's a discipline slicing from watching history. That's like saying promoting history or biology or mathematics. What does that mean? When I pointed out *that the total population here is about 2 percent of the country. How can this tiny percentage impose the Shariah on 98 percent of the population?*

COOPER: *Unfortunately, we've got to go. (End of Interview)*

This dialogue just about sums up the divide between empty hype and rhetoric presented by Islamophobes, and between academic facts and figures presented by educated individuals. Anyone with an iota of intelligence can tell what is right and what is wrong. It's just a case of looking for the truth, and not listening to the hype and distractions.

Frequently Asked Questions about Islam

From time to time, I get e-mails in my inbox with seemingly evolved questions. It is apparent that people have put their mind towards posing questions to Muslims that they may find difficult to respond to. This chapter is dedicated to such questions, and the answer to those questions will also be provided.

Who or what is Allah?

Allah is simply the Arabic name for God. Did you know that even Arab Christians use the word *Allah* for God?

Even Jesus have used a word similar to *Allah* as he spoke a language called Aramaic, and in that language the name of God is AaLaH, according to an Aramaic dictionary.[70]

So just like Spanish call God *Dios,* and the French call God *Dieu,* and the Germans call God *Gott,* Arabs call God *Allah.*

What is the difference between Sunni and Shia Muslims?

After the Prophet Muhammad (peace be upon him,)passed away, there was a difference of opinion amongst his followers as to who should lead the Muslims. The majority of the Muslims decided that his life-long ally and friend Abu Bakr should lead

---

[70] http://www.atour.com/dictionary/

the Muslims. However, a minority decided that because Ali was a blood relative of Prophet Muhammad, and also his son-in-law, he had more right to the leadership position. This minority group became the *Shia*. *Shia* in Arabic means "splinter group", because they split away from the majority of Muslims who pledged allegiance to Abu Bakr. The *Shia* are approximately 5% of the world's Muslim population.

Why do Muslim women cover the way that they do?

From the beginning of time, both men and women have been ordered to cover their bodies by God. Even the Bible talks about women dressing modestly, in the following two verses:

I also want women to dress modestly, with decency and propriety, not with braided hair or gold or pearls or expensive clothes, but with good deeds, appropriate for women who profess to worship God.[71]

Your beauty should not come from outward adornment, such as braided hair and the wearing of gold jewelry and fine clothes. Instead, it should be that of your inner self, the unfading beauty of a gentle and quiet spirit, which is of great worth in God's sight. For this is the way the holy women of the past who put their hope in God used to make themselves beautiful.[72]

Also, if we look at all images and statues of the Virgin Mary, we will find her mode of dress to be exactly the same as Muslim

---

[71] NIV, 1 Timothy 2:9-10
[72] NIV, 1 Peter 3:2-5

women today. Even 100 years ago in Western society, women made a point of wearing a bonnet over their heads before leaving the house, and wore long skirts; the showing of an ankle was even regarded as a taboo.

Muslim women have continued to maintain that modesty. It enables them to be judged not for their looks or how short or long their skirt is, but for their character and intelligence.

Why do Muslims pray five times a day?

Firstly, we pray 5 times daily because it is a command of God to do so.

Secondly, it gives us a constant reminder about the reason for our creation, which is to serve God at all times, and not just one day of the week.

It also helps us to refrain from sins, as we would be ashamed to stand in front of God for prayer because of the sin we committed. So this fact alone compels us to avoid indulging in sins in between the prayers.

Why do Muslims encourage polygamy?

Islam doesn't encourage polygamy; it simply allows (and also restricts) polygamy, if certain criteria are met. In countries where polygamy is against the law, Muslims are instructed to abide by the law of that country.

Muslims derive the permissibility of polygamy in Islam from the *Qur'anic* verse:

"If you fear that you shall not be able to deal justly with the orphans, marry women of your choice, two, or three, or four; but if you fear that you shall not be able to deal justly (with them), then (marry) only one..." [73]

From this verse, it is evident that polygamy is neither mandatory, nor encouraged, but merely permitted. The *Qur'an* also warns about the difficulty of dealing justly between multiple wives:

"Ye are never able to be fair and just as between women, even if it is your ardent desire: But turn not away (from a woman) altogether, so as to leave her (as it were) hanging (in the air). If ye come to a friendly understanding, and practice self-restraint, God is Oft-forgiving, Most Merciful." [74]

Nevertheless, it ordained fair and equitable dealing with wives an obligation. If one is not sure of being able to deal justly with wives, the *Qur'an* says: *"then (marry) only one"* [75]

The *Qur'anic* injunction, thus, made polygamy restrictive, when compared with the prevalent practice in the world.

Dr. Jamal Badawi, a Canadian Islamic scholar says:

---

[73] The Holy *Qur'an*, Chapter 4, Verse 3.
[74] The Holy Qur'an, Chapter 4, Verse 129
[75] The Holy Quran, Chapter 4, Verse 9

"The requirement of justice rules out the fantasy that man can "own as many as he pleases." It also rules out the concept of a "secondary wife", for all wives have exactly the same status and are entitled to identical rights and claims over their husband. It also implies, according to the Islamic Law, that should the husband fail to provide enough support for any of his wives, she can go to court and ask for a divorce."[76]

The question that also arises is: "Did the institution of polygamy originate in Islam"? A brief look at major world religions and cultures clearly indicates that this is not the case.

Polygamy is permitted in Judaism. According to Talmudic law, Abraham had three wives, and Solomon had hundreds of wives. The practice of polygamy continued in Judaism until Rabbi Gershom ben Yehudah (960 C.E to 1030 C.E) issued an edict against it. The Jewish Sephardic communities living in Muslim countries continued the practice up to as late as 1950, when an Act of the Chief Rabbinate of Israel extended the ban on marrying more than one wife.

There is no passage in the New Testament that expressly prohibits polygamy except in the case of bishops and deacons. This was the understanding of the early Church Fathers and for several centuries in the Christian era.

---

[76] http://www.islamicweb.com/begin/gender.pdf

Westermarck, a noted authority on the history of human marriages states: "On various occasions Luther speaks of polygamy with considerable toleration. It had not been forbidden by God: even Abraham, who was a "perfect Christian", had two wives. It is true that God had allowed such marriages to certain men of the Old Testament only in particular circumstances, and if a Christian wanted to follow their example he had to show that the circumstances were similar in his case; but polygamy was undoubtedly preferable to divorce. In 1650, soon after the Peace of Westphalia, when the population had been greatly reduced by the Thirty Years' War, the Frankish Kreistag at Nuremberg passed a resolution that thenceforth every man should be allowed to marry two women. Certain sects of Christians have even advocated polygamy with much fervor. In 1531 the Anabaptists openly preached at Munster that he who wants to be a true Christian must have several wives. And the Mormons, as the entire world knows, regard polygamy as a divine institution."[77]

St. Augustine also is said to have favored polygamy. He is quoted:

"That the holy fathers of olden times after Abraham, and before him, to whom God gave His testimony that "they pleased Him," [Heb. 11:4-6] thus used their wives, no one who is a Christian ought to doubt, since it was permitted to certain individuals amongst them to have a plurality

---

[77] Westermarck, Edward; History of Human Marriage

of wives, where the reason was for the multiplication of their offspring, not the desire of varying gratification. In the advance, however, of the human race, it came to pass that to certain good men were united a plurality of good wives, --- many to each; and from this it would seem that moderation sought rather unity on one side for dignity, while nature permitted plurality on the other side for fecundity. For on natural principles it is more feasible for one to have dominion over many, than for many to have dominion over one "[78]

According to Father Eugene Hillman in his book, *Polygamy Reconsidered*, he says, *"Nowhere in the New Testament is there any explicit commandment that marriage should be monogamous or any explicit commandment forbidding polygamy."*

Many Hindu religious personalities, according to their scriptures, had multiple wives. King Dashrat, the father of Rama, had more than one wife. Krishna, another key Hindu figurehead, had several wives.

Let us consider a few honest questions: What is the situation in countries that have banned polygamy? Do they really enjoy sincere and faithful "monogamy" as the norm? Are infidelity and secret extramarital sexual relationships more moral than the legitimate, legally protected husband-wife relationships practiced under polygamy? if there is a pressing need for it.

---

[78] A Select Library of the Nicene and Post-Nicene Fathers of The Christian Church, Volume 5, page 267

[79] Eugene Hillman, Polygamy Reconsidered: African Plural Marriage and the Christian Churches p. 140.

which of the two situations is better? We have lost count of the number of times politicians (even "moral" conservative politicians), athletes, and actors are in the news for having extra-marital affairs, resulting in the subsequent break-up of their families.

There are also some societies where women outnumber men. Sometimes, wars take a heavier toll on men as compared to women. For unmarried women who cannot find husbands and widows who aspire to a respectable family life, polygamy is often an acceptable alternative.

The association of polygamy only with the religion of Islam is a serious misunderstanding. Polygamy was practiced, often without limitations, in almost all cultures. In Islam, polygamy is not a substitute for monogamy, but merely a permission to practice limited polygamy, which is consistent with Islam's realistic view of human nature, as well as social needs.[80]

Karen Armstrong is a renowned historian, who has written many books about Islam. She writes about the controversial subject of polygamy in her book *Muhammad: A Prophet for our Times*:

"Each of the Muslim dead had left wives and daughters without protectors. After the defeat, a revelation came to Muhammad giving Muslims permission to take four wives. Muslims must

---

[80]Taken from www.whyislam.org with some editing.

remember that God had created men and women from a single living entity, so that both sexes were equally precious in his sight." (pg. 145)

"The institution of polygamy has been much criticized as the source of considerable suffering for Muslim women, but at the time of this revelation it constituted a social advance. In the pre-Islamic period, both men and women were allowed several spouses. After marriage, a woman remained at the home of her family, and was visited by all her "husbands." It was, in effect, a form of licensed prostitution." (pg. 145) Islam banned polyandry, meaning a woman having several husbands, and limited the polygamy, which had no limit prior to Islam, to four wives.

"The Qur'anic institution of polygamy was a piece of social legislation. It was designed not to gratify the male sexual appetite, but to correct the injustices done to widows, orphans and other female dependents, which were especially vulnerable." (pg. 147)

"Polygamy was designed to ensure that unprotected women would be decently married, and to abolish the old loose, irresponsible liaisons; men could have only four wives and must treat them equitably; it was an unjustifiably wicked act to devour their property." (pg. 147)

"The Qur'an was attempting to give women a legal status that most Western women would not enjoy until the 19th century.

The emancipation of women was a project dear to the Prophet's heart, but it was resolutely opposed by many men in the *ummah*, including some of his closest companions." (pg. 147)

Does the *Qur'an* say that the Earth is flat?

The reason that some people ask this question is that the Qur'an says that "God has made the earth for you as a carpet". This gives an indication that the earth is flat. Does this not contradict established modern science? The question refers to a verse from the Qur'an in Surah Nuh: "And God has made the earth for you as a carpet (spread out)."[81]

But the sentence in the above verse is not complete. It continues in the next verse, explaining the previous verse. It says: "That ye may go about therein, in spacious roads."[82] A similar message is repeated in Surah TaHa: "He Who has made for you the earth like a carpet spread out; has enabled you to go about therein by roads (and channels)...."[83]

The surface of the earth (i.e. the earth's crust) is less than 30 miles in thickness and is relatively very thin compared to the radius of the earth which is about 3750 miles. The deeper layers of the earth are very hot, fluid and hostile to any form of life.

---

[81] The Holy Qur'an, Chapter 71, Verse 19
[82] The Holy *Qur'an*, Chapter 71, Verse 20
[83] The Holy *Qur'an*, Chapter 20-Verse 53

The earth's crust is a solidified shell on which we can live. The Qur'an rightly refers to it like a carpet spread out, so that we can travel along its roads and paths.

Not a single verse of the Qur'an says that the earth is flat. The Qur'an only compares the earth's crust with a carpet. Some people seem to think that carpet can only be put on an absolute flat surface. It is possible to spread a carpet on a large sphere such as the earth. It can easily be demonstrated by taking a huge model of the earth's globe covering it with a carpet.

Carpet is generally put on any type of surface that is not very comfortable to walk on. The Qur'an describes the earth's crust as a carpet, without which human beings would not be able to survive because of the hot, fluid and hostile environment beneath it. The Qur'an is thus not only logical, it is mentioning a scientific fact that was discovered by geologists centuries later.

Similarly, the Qur'an says in several verses that the earth has been spread out.

"And We have spread out the (spacious) earth: how excellently We do spread out!"[84]

Similarly the Qur'an also mentions in several other verses that the earth is an expanse:

---

[84] The Holy *Qur'an*, Chapter 51, Verse 48

"Have We not made the earth as a wide expanse. And the mountains as pegs?"[85]

None of these verses of the Qur'an contain even the slightest indication, implied or otherwise, that the earth is flat. It only indicates that the earth is spacious and the reason for this spaciousness of the earth is mentioned. The Glorious Qur'an says:

"O My servants who believe! Truly, spacious is My Earth: therefore serve you Me (And Me alone)!"[86] Therefore none can give the excuse, that he could not do good and was forced to do evil because of the surroundings and circumstances.

The Qur'an mentions the actual shape of the earth in the following verse: "And we have made the earth egg shaped".[87] The Arabic word Dahaha means egg shaped. It also means an expanse. Dahaha is derived from Duhiya which specifically refers to the egg of an ostrich which is geo-spherical in shape, exactly like the shape of the earth.

Thus the Qur'an and modern established science are in perfect harmony, and do not contradict each other.

---

[85] The Holy Qur'an, Chapter 78, Verse 6-7
[86] The Holy Qur'an, Chapter 29, Verse 56
[87] The Holy Qur'an, Chapter 79, Verse 30

Why don't Muslims eat pork?

First and foremost, we don't eat pork because God commands us not to:

"Forbidden to you (for food) are: dead meat, blood, the flesh of swine, and that on which hath been invoked the name of other than God."[88]

The prohibition from pork is not limited to the Islamic faith. It was also prohibited in previous scriptures.

The Bible prohibits the consumption of pork, in the book of Leviticus:

"And the swine, though he divide the hoof, and be cloven footed, yet he cheweth not the cud; he is unclean to you".

"Of their flesh shall ye not eat, and their carcass shall ye not touch, they are unclean to you."[89]

Pork is also prohibited in the Bible in the book of Deuteronomy:

"And the swine, because it divideth the hoof, yet cheweth not the cud, it is unclean unto you. Ye shall not eat of their flesh, nor touch their dead carcass."[90]

A similar prohibition is repeated in the Bible in the book of Isaiah:

---

[88] The Holy *Qur'an*; Surah 5, Verse 3
[89] Leviticus 11:7-8
[90] Deuteronomy 14:8

"I have spread out my hands all the day unto a rebellious people, which walketh in a way that was not good, after their own thoughts; A people that provoketh me to anger continually to my face; that sacrificeth in gardens, and burneth incense upon altars of brick; Which remain among the graves, and lodge in the monuments, which eat swine's flesh, and broth of abominable things is in their vessels."[91]

Most Christians don't observe these dietary laws because of various, sometimes vague, theological reasons. In fact, when Joel Osteen, evangelical best-selling author and preacher declared pork was off limits and he publicly declared in a sermon that he didn't eat pork, he was heavily criticized for his stance by many different denominations of Christianity.

However, Muslims believe that rules of God have been consistent through all Prophetic teachings, and continue to maintain the strict guidelines of dietary law.

What does the word jihad mean?

The real meaning of this word is "to struggle". There are many ways that a person engages in "jihad". One rule is trying to live a right to lifestyle despite difficult odds eased engaging in jihad. One is trying to raise his children in their best possible way to try to live morally and honestly is engaging in jihad. A person who is trying to put food on the table for his family is performing jihad. Also, within the scope of the meaning of

---

[91] Isaiah 65:2-5

Jihad, is also to engage in fighting when the need dictates, to protect one's country, religion, or family.

However there are strict rules and regulations to this fighting:

The *Qur'an* has clearly restricted this type of jihad to certain conditions while forbidding transgression of any sort.

"(Fighting is) permitted to those who are fought against, because they have been wronged. Surely God is able to give them victory. Those who have been driven from their homes unjustly only because they said: "Our Lord is God." If God had not repelled some people by means of others, cloisters and churches and synagogues and mosques, wherein the Name of God is much mentioned, would assuredly have been pulled down. God helps one who helps Him [His religion]. Surely God is All-Strong, All-Mighty. Those who, if We give them power in the land, establish worship and pay the poor-due and enjoin the good and forbid the evil. And God's is the sequel of events."[92]

1. The battle can only be defensive and not an offensive one. *And fight in the cause of God against those who fight against you, but do not transgress. Surely God loves not the transgressors.[93]*

2. Muslims should face oppression in the practice of their religion and when it is a threat to their life.

---

[92] The Holy *Qur'an* Chapter 22, verses 39-41.
[93] The Holy *Qur'an*, Surah 2, Verse 191

3. Muslims who have been driven out of their homes; the teaching is to initially leave from where the oppression is taking place, and if the oppressor attacks the Muslims to stop them from the practice of their religion in the new abode and also threaten their lives, only in these circumstances are the Muslims allowed to take up arms in a defensive battle.

More verses from the Qur'an highlighting the above points will be mentioned later in the book.

Furthermore, there are clear directions in what can and cannot be done in a battle fought by the Muslims.

1. Civilians who are not fighting against Muslims are not to be attacked or killed at all.
2. Crops or other sources of food and water and cattle or other animals are not to be destroyed.
3. Hospitals, orphanages and other places of safety and refuge are not to be destroyed.
4. Mosques, churches, synagogues and other places of worship are not to be destroyed.
5. Women, children, old and disabled are to be left untouched.
6. If the aggressor stops the aggression or offers a treaty it should be accepted and the fighting stopped forthwith.

7. Fleeing oppressors need not be pursued to any unnecessary length and should be allowed to return to their home.

8. Prisoners of War should be treated with respect and their basic needs be fulfilled and they should be freed or ransomed as soon as possible after the battle.

Bear in mind that these rulings were introduced over a millennia before the Geneva Convention.

Hence it is very clear that the purpose of any such battle is to restore peace and not to promote aggression. It is important to note that starting of such a battle is not in the hands of the Muslims but can only be initiated by an oppressor fulfilling the aforementioned conditions.

Prophet Muhammad spent the first 13 years of prophet hood in Mecca striving to spread the message of *Qur'an* against intense and fierce oppression but he never raised a finger in response. He left Mecca for Madinah but the Meccans continued to pursue him in Madinah. It was only when they launched a battle to kill Muslims in Madinah that a physical battle in self-defense was permitted and even then only to the extent to preserve their freedom to live in peace and to worship God.[94]

---

[94] www.islamfaq.org

In fact, the *Qur'an* explains that the allowance of fighting was given to people who had been oppressed and fought against, and also to protect places of worship, including churches and synagogues, has been sanctioned by God throughout history.

"Permission (to fight) is given to those against whom fighting is launched, because they have been wronged, and God is powerful to give them victory. They are) the ones who were expelled from their homes without any just reason, except that they say "Our Lord is God." Had God not been repelling some people by means of some others, the monasteries, the churches, the synagogues and the mosques where God's name is abundantly recited would have been demolished. God will definitely help those who help Him (by defending the religion prescribed by Him.) Surely God is Powerful, Mighty. The ones who help God are) those who, when We give them power in the land, establish Salah, pay Zakah, bid what is Fair and forbid what is Unfair. And with God lies the fate of all matters." [95]

This verse clearly shows that all religions in the past had to deal with attacks, and had to stand up to defend their religion, their families, and their communities, otherwise they would have all been destroyed, including their holy sanctuaries, their monasteries, churches and synagogues. There are a lot of references in the Bible to warfare, which anyone can look up.

---

[95] The Holy *Qur'an*, Surah 22, verses 39-41.

Also, keep in mind that the ruling on bearing arms came about fourteen years after Prophet Muhammad *(peace be upon him)* started preaching the message of Islam, and even that was due to the Quraish becoming a hindrance in propagating the message of Islam.

Do Islam and Christianity have different origins?

Together with Judaism, Islam and Christianity go back to the prophet and patriarch Abraham, and the three prophets, Moses, Jesus, and Muhammad, peace be upon them all, are directly descended from his sons; Muhammad *(peace be upon him)* from the eldest, Ishmael, and Moses and Jesus, from Isaac. Abraham established the settlement, which today is the city of Meccah, and built the Kabah towards which all Muslims turn when they pray. This story is found in the book of Genesis in the Old Testament.

What is the Kabah?

The Kabah is the place of worship, which God commanded Abraham and Ishmael to build over four thousand years ago. The building was constructed of stone on what many believe was the original site of a sanctuary established by Adam. God commanded Abraham to summon all mankind to visit this place, and when pilgrims go there today they say 'At Thy service, O Lord', in response to Abraham's summons. The *Qur'an* describes the *Ka'aba* as "the first house (of worship) built for mankind".

Ka'aba is the Qibla i.e. the direction Muslims face during their prayers. It is important to note that though Muslims face the

Ka'aba during prayers, they do not worship the *Ka'aba*. Muslims worship and bow to none but Allah.

"We see the turning of thy face (for guidance) to the heavens: now shall We turn thee to a Qiblah that shall please thee. Turn then thy face in the direction of the Sacred Mosque: wherever ye are, turn your faces in that direction."[96]

Islam believes in fostering unity

For instance, if Muslims want to offer Salaah (Prayer), it is possible that some may wish to face north, while some may wish to face south. In order to unite Muslims in their worship of the One True God, Muslims, wherever they may be, are asked to face in only one direction i.e. towards the *Ka'aba*. If some Muslims live towards the west of the *Ka'aba* they face the east. Similarly if they live towards the east of the *Ka'aba* they face the west.

Tawaaf around *Ka'aba* is to indicate the Oneness of God

When the Muslims go to Masjid-e-*Haraam* in Meccah, they perform tawaaf or circumambulation round the *Ka'aba*. This act symbolizes the belief and worship of One God, since, just as every circle has one center, so also there is only one Allah worthy of worship. This circumambulation emulates the angels

---

[96] The Holy *Qur'an*, Chapter 2, Verse 144

that go around the *arsh* or the throne of God in the heavens directly above the *Ka'aba*.

Hadith of Umar (may Allah be pleased with him)

People often ask about the significance of the Black Stone, saying that kissing it and revering it is tantamount to idol-worship. Regarding the black stone, hajr-e-aswad, there is a hadith (tradition), attributed to the illustrious companion of the Prophet Muhammad, Umar (may Allah be pleased with him).

According to Sahih Bukhari, Volume 2, book of Hajj, chapter 56, Hadith.No. 675. Umar (may Allah be pleased with him) said, "I know that you are a stone and can neither benefit nor harm. Had I not seen the Prophet (pbuh) touching (and kissing) you, I would never have touched (and kissed) you".

To summarize, all Muslims face the *Ka'aba* to pray, not because they worship the building, but as a show of unity, and symbolic gesture of focusing towards one God.

How exactly did Muhammad die? (Was he or was he not poisoned by a Jewish woman?) Wouldn't a prophet know he was going to be harmed?

Not necessarily. We believe that all Messengers sent by God were human beings. From that perspective, they could not know things that were hidden, unless and until God himself informed them. The *Qur'an* emphasizes that Prophet Muhammad (PBUH) doesn't know unseen or hidden things (called ghaib in Arabic), unless he was informed by the angel Gabriel or God himself.[97] As for the issue of the Jewish woman poisoning him, he didn't actually die from that poison, but it did affect him until the end of his life, as it made him sick from time to time. He ultimately died a natural death, at the age of 63 years old.

Do men receive 72 virgins and young boys once in paradise (heaven)?

Paradise is a place of happiness and bliss, and anyone can have whatever they want, whether they want 72 or 7200, it's up to them. Keep in mind that we cannot imagine how Paradise will be, and we can only compare it to what we see in this world. This is based on the saying of the prophet Muhammad. Abu Hurairah (May God be pleased with him) said: The Messenger of God said, "God, the Exalted, has said: `I have prepared for my righteous servants what no eye has seen, no ear has heard, and the mind of no man has conceived.' If you wish, recite: "No person knows what is kept hidden for them of joy as a reward for what they used to do." (The Holy *Qur'an*, 32:17)[98]

---

[97] The Holy *Qur'an,* Chapter 7, Verse 188.
[98] Al-Bukhari and Muslim

Your question of "young boys" seems to be implying that one would sexually derive pleasure from them. This has never been understood from classical texts. The understanding is they will be servants to serve the dwellers of paradise.

What do women receive in paradise (heaven)?

Anything they want, just like men!

When a Christian couple marries their marriage is valid according to the law and of Christian standards here, if the woman decides to convert to Islam is their marriage still valid? If not, why and according to whom?

When a Christian woman converts to Islam, her marriage to her Christian husband is invalidated Islamically. The reason for this is that a Muslim woman cannot be married to a non-Muslim man. We don't enforce this ruling as Muslims in the United States, as we have no legal basis to do so, because Islamic law (*Shariah*) doesn't apply in this country, contrary to popular myths that are prevalent nowadays. However, legally, according to American law, the marriage is still intact, and they would have to go to a court and go through legal proceedings to have the marriage annulled.

Other rulings related to this subject are as follows:

1. A Muslim is allowed to marry a Christian or Jewish woman.

2. If a Christian couple converts to Islam at the same time, their Christian marriage would be valid according to Islamic teachings, and they would not need to remarry according to the Islamic tradition.

God is not a hypocrite and does not go back on his word. That being fact, why would Muhammad command that men can only have up to 4 wives, yet for him he was able to have more than one and others as well?

The issue of polygamy as a whole is misunderstood by non-Muslims. Polygamy was very common and prior to Islam there was no limit to the wives that one could have. Islam set a maximum of four wives for men. Why did the prophet Muhammad have more than four wives? Because in the days of the Prophet, marrying in to a certain tribe had political ramifications. The new tribe became your family and therefore they would be more inclined to listen to your message. This was the main reason. Bear in mind also that all except one of his wives were either divorcees or widows. Also worth noting is that nobody at that time objected to his multiple wives because polygamy was the norm. Only in recent times it has become an issue, because society as a whole is not used to polygamy, and also each and every action of the prophet Muhammad has come under scrutiny from critics who want to malign Islam by assassinating the character of the messenger.

If you are married and have sex with another person and you are caught according to Islam what happens?

The ruling for adultery, or any sin for that matter, is that a person should repent to God in privacy, without exposing that sin to others. That is also a ruling that is derived from the Qur'an:

"And they (the pious slaves of God) do not call to any other god except for God himself and they don't kill any soul that God has prohibited except with the right (meaning capital punishment for a crime) and they don't commit adultery. Whoever commits this act falls into sin. Punishment will be multiplied for him on the Day of Judgment and he will stay in it in the state of disgrace. **Except he who repents and has faith and he does good deeds, for such people God will turn their sins into good deeds. And indeed God is forgiving merciful.**"[99]

In the above verses of the Qur'an, we see that God not only forgives the sin, but changes the sin into good deeds. If we look at events that took place in life of the prophet Muhammad, we will find that people came to him and admitted committing adultery, and he used to have them dragged away from him. From such references we can derive that the best course of action is for a person to have penitence and turn to his Lord and ask forgiveness. If he does that, then he will, God willing, be forgiven.

---

[99] The Holy Qur'an, Surah al-Furqan 25:v-68-70

The alternative ruling on adultery is that a person is stoned to death if he is married, but you must have four witnesses. Who has sex in a place where there are four witnesses? So it's impossible to prove, and rarely occurs. In addition to the ruling of four witnesses, the witnesses that testify against the adulterer are also under the threat of being punished by 80 lashes is their testimony is found to be false. This will also be the case if three come forward, and they don't have a fourth witness. Or if there were originally four witnesses, and one or more back out from testifying. So this threat of punishment is a deterrent for witnesses that they should not come forward with such testimony that blemishes the honor and standing of an individual in society.

To summarize, the best course of action for the adulterer is to seek forgiveness directly from God, as punishment in the form of stoning is almost impossible to implement because of the strict conditions applicable to it.

If we look at the Bible, we will find almost similar rulings. For example, the book of Deuteronomy has the punishment of stoning mentioned in it, not only for adultery, but for other reasons also:

1. Breaking the Shabbat (Numbers 15:32-36)
2. Giving one's "seed" (offspring) "to Moloch" (the name of an Idol) in a sacrifice (Leviticus 20:2)

3. Having a "familiar spirit" (or being a necromancer) or being a "wizard" (Lev. 20:27)

4. Cursing God (Lev. 24:10-16)

5. Engaging in idolatry (Deuteronomy 17:2-7) or encouraging others to do so (Deut. 13:7-12)

6. Rebellion against parents (Deut. 21,21)

7. Getting married as though a virgin, when not a virgin (Deut. 22:13-21)

8. Sexual intercourse between a man and a woman engaged to another man (both should be stoned, Deut. 22:23-24)[100]

As we can see from the above references in the Old Testament, stoning was a punishment that was given for the smallest of things when compared with the Islamic ruling on the bigger sin of adultery. The prohibition of adultery is after all one of the 10 Commandments; Thou shalt not commit adultery.[101]

The forgiveness aspect of the Islamic faith is comparable to the story of Jesus when he told his followers who were about to stone an adulteress that "let he who has no sin cast the first stone."[102]

---

[100] http://en.wikipedia.org/wiki/Stoning

[101] Exodus 20:14

[102] John 8:7 King James Bible, "So when they continued asking him, he lifted himself up, and said unto them, He that is without sin among you, let him first cast a stone at her."

Similar sayings are demonstrated in the teachings of the Prophet Muhammad:

`Abdullah bin Mas`ud (May Allah be pleased with him) reported: A man kissed a woman and he came to the Prophet and made a mention of that to him. It was (on this occasion) that this verse was revealed:

"And perform Prayer at the two ends of the day and in some hours of the night [i.e., the five compulsory Prayers]. Verily, the good deeds remove the evil deeds".[103]

That person said, "O Messenger of Allah, does it concern me only?". He said, "It concerns the whole of my *Ummah* (nation)".[104]

Anas bin Malik reported: A man came to the Prophet and said, "O Messenger of Allah, I have committed a sin liable of ordained punishment. So execute punishment on me". Messenger of Allah did not ask him about it, and then came the (time for) Prayer. So he performed Prayer with Messenger of Allah When Messenger of Allah finished Prayer, the man stood up and said: "O Messenger of Allah! I have committed a sin. So execute the Ordinance of Allah upon me". He asked, "Have you

---

[103] The Holy Quran, Chapter 11, Verse 114
[104] Bukhari and Muslim

performed Prayer with us?" "Yes", he replied. Messenger of Allah said, "Verily, Allah has forgiven you".[105]

The person who had committed the sin came to the Prophet to seek punishment for his wrongdoing is said to have been Abul-Yusr Ka`b bin `Amr whose story was also mentioned in the previous Hadith. The sin that he committed was one that would have made him legally deserving of punishment, but the Prophet Muhammad told him that his sin was forgiven through the virtue of prayers. This shows that repentance towards God is encouraged in Islam, not physical punishment.

So in essence, Islam combined Judaic and Christian teachings to come up with the punishment of stoning if the criteria of the four witnesses is fulfilled (which is almost impossible), and more encouragement towards repentance and subsequent forgiveness for a person to make peace with his Lord in solitude.

Why would Muhammad marry a young girl?

This is another myth spread to give Muhammad a bad name. The reference is obviously to the Prophet Muhammad marrying Aisha, his youngest wife. The reality is as follows:

1. She was the only one of the wives of the Prophet to be a virgin at marriage. The rest of his wives were widows and divorcees. If he was lusting after young women, he

---

[105] Bukhari and Muslim

could have married the youngest women, and people would have readily given their daughters in marriage to him. But he didn't.

2. The first wife the prophet married was 40 years old and he was 25. Although one would usually marry someone younger

3. He did not marry anyone while married to Khadija (the whole 25 years).

4. The second time he got married, he was 50 and he married Sawda who was around 80 years old.

5. Aisha was young and bright and memorized every detail about what the prophet said and had done during their lifetime together and especially personal details about the prophets life style at home. This was one of the main reason he married a young person who could learn all this and teach it to everyone after his passing, and she did

6. As for the controversy surrounding her age, it is known that between the marriage contract and Aisha's moving to the Prophet's household, there was a 3-year gap during which she stayed with her parents.

7. It is also known that her moving to the Prophet's household took place in the first or second year after migration from Mecca to Madinah.

8. It is also known that the Meccan period lasted for 13 years, and the famous biographer Ibn Ishaq lists the name of Aisha among the very early persons who

accepted Islam in the first few months of the Prophet's mission. If we were to add a minimum age of Aisha to understand what she was accepting, say 4 + the 13 years in Mecca+ 1 or 2 years in Madinah, it adds up probably to 19 years and not only 9, which is the number reported in Al-Bukhari.

9. While the above is more than enough, it is noted also that many historians have debated the age of Aisha when she married the Prophet (peace and blessings be upon him). One is that some say that Aisha died at the age of 50 after migration(from Mecca to Madinah), at the age of 67, which means that she was born 17 years old before migration and since her marriage was consummated one or two years after migration, it must have taken place at the age of 19.

10. It is also known that her sister Asmaa was 10 years her senior. It is interesting to note that Asmaa died in the year 73 after migration, at the age of 100, this means she was born 27 years before migration (100-73). Since she was 10 years older, then Aisha was born 17 years before migration, which is consistent with these other reports.

Karen Armstrong, a non-Muslim historian who has studied the life of the Prophet Muhammad in detail, says in her book, *Muhammad: A Prophet for Our Time:*

"There was no impropriety in Muhammad's betrothal to 'A'isha. Marriages conducted in absentia to seal an alliance were often contracted at this time between adults and minors who were even younger than 'A'isha. This practice continued in Europe well into the early modern period. There was no question of consummating the marriage until 'A'isha reached puberty, when she would have been married off like any other girl."[106]

It is said that women should dress modestly, what is considered "modest"?

Modest means loose-fitting and covering the whole body, except face and hands. Both the Old Testament and New Testament rulings related to dress.

According to the Old Testament, "In like manner also, that women adorn themselves in modest apparel, with shamefacedness and sobriety; not with broided hair, or gold, or pearls, or costly array."[107]

The Bible also prohibits people from dressing similarly to the opposite gender, which is similar to the teachings of Islam. "A woman must not wear men's clothing, nor a man wear

---

[106] Karen Armstrong, *Muhammad: A Prophet for our time, p-109*
[107] Timothy 2:9 King James Version

women's clothing, for the LORD your God detests anyone who does this."[108]

According to a saying of the prophet Muhammad, "The Prophet cursed men who wear women's clothing and women who wear men's."[109]

According to the New Testament, when engaged in religious worship, both men and women are instructed to dress modestly:

"Any man who prays or prophesies with something on his head disgraces his head, but any woman who prays or prophesies with her head unveiled disgraces her head--it is one and the same thing as having her head shaved. For if a woman will not veil herself, then she should cut off her hair; but if it is disgraceful for a woman to have her hair cut off or to be shaved, she should wear a veil. For a man ought not to have his head veiled, since he is the image and reflection of God; but woman is the reflection of man."[110]

As we can see, in Judeo-Christian teaching we find similarities between the dress code taught to Muslims. The only difference is that Muslims take the teachings very literally and implement them in their lives, whereas other faith groups do not take the rulings in such a literal way.

---

[108] NIV, Deuteronomy 22:5
[109] Abu Dawud
[110] NRSV, 1 Corinthians 11:4-7

Can Muslim women wear Western dress? If the clothing, blouse and pants were loose then it would be fine. Contrary to popular understanding, Muslim men are also commanded to wear modest and loose clothing.

Did Muhammad write the *Qur'an* personally, if he did not then who did?

No, he didn't write it personally, because he couldn't read or write. One thing that people do not keep in mind is that right from the very beginning the *Qur'an* was preserved by putting it to memory. Even to this day the first line of defense in protecting the *Qur'an* is memorizing it, and there are tens of thousands of Muslims worldwide, some as young as five or six years old, that have dedicated the *Qur'an* to memory verbatim, word for word. Writing the *Qur'an* was a secondary method of preservation, and memory was the first way. The *Qur'an* was also written in its complete form, before the death of the Prophet, but put in the shape of a book after the death of the prophet Muhammad. The actual reason that it was put into book form at that time was that there was a danger that all the people that have memorized it would die out, and there would be no way to retrieve the memorized portions of the *Qur'an*. So it was written down as a backup rather than original method of preservation, which is still prevalent today, memorization.

What is the purpose of the Hadith if the *Qur'an* is perfect and complete?

Hadith means the sayings and actions of the Prophet Muhammad, which complement the teachings of the *Qur'an*. [111]The purpose of the *Hadith* is explaining and clarifying the purpose behind the verses of the *Qur'an*, and that is actually commanded to us in the *Qur'an*, to follow and obey the Prophet. For example the *Qur'an* tells us to pray, but details of it are in hadith. The same thing applies for hajj, zakat etc.

---

[111] See The Holy *Qur'an* Surah Nahl, Verse 44,

Accusations against the reliability of the *Qur'an*

Many critics allege that Prophet Muhammad himself was not the author of the *Qur'an* but he learnt it and/or plagiarized (copied or adapted) it from other human sources or from previous scriptures or revelations. Here is a list of those accusations, and the response to them.[112]

"Muhammad learnt the *Qur'an* from a Roman Blacksmith who was a Christian"

Some Pagans accused the Prophet of learning the *Qur'an* from a Roman Blacksmith, who was a Christian staying at the outskirts of Mecca.

The Prophet very often used to go and watch him do his work. A revelation of the *Qur'an* was sufficient to dismiss this charge - the *Qur'an* says in Surah An-Nahl chapter 16 verse 103:

"We know indeed that they say, 'It is a man that teaches him,' The tongue of him they wickedly point to is notably foreign, while this is Arabic, pure and clear."[113]

How could a person whose mother tongue was foreign and could hardly speak little but of poor broken Arabic be the

---

[112] www.islam.thetruecall.com with editing.
[113] The Holy Quran, Chapter 16, Verse 103

source of the *Qur'an* which is pure, eloquent, fine Arabic? To believe that the blacksmith taught the Prophet the *Qur'an* is somewhat similar to believing that a Chinese immigrant to England, who did not know proper English, taught Shakespeare.

"Muhammad learnt from Waraqa - The Relative Of Khadijah"

Muhammad's contacts with the Jewish and Christian Scholars were very limited. The most prominent Christian known to him was an old blind man called Waraqa ibn-Naufal who was a relative of the Prophet's first wife Khadijah. Although of Arab descent, he was a convert to Christianity and was very well versed with the New Testament. The Prophet only met him twice, first when Waraqa was worshipping at the *Ka'aba* (before the Prophetic Mission) and he kissed the Prophet's forehead affectionately. The second occasion was when the Prophet went to meet Waraqa accompanied by his wife Khadija after receiving the first revelation. Waraqa died three years later and the revelation continued for about 23 years. It is therefore ridiculous to assume that Waraqa was the source of the contents of the *Qur'an*, as he died at the very beginning of the Prophethood.

"Prophet learnt the *Qur'an* from having religious discussions with the Jews and Christians"

It is true that the Prophet did have religious discussions with the Jews and Christians but they took place in Madinah more than 13 years after the revelation of the *Qur'an* had started. The allegation that these Jews and Christians were the source of the *Qur'an* is inconceivable, since in these discussions Prophet Muhammad was performing the roles of a teacher and of a preacher while inviting them to embrace Islam and pointing out that they had deviated from their true teachings of Monotheism. Several of these Jews and Christians later embraced Islam.

"The Prophet learnt the *Qur'an* from those Jews and Christians that he met outside Arabia"

All historical records available show that Muhammad had made only three trips outside Meccah before his Prophethood:

1. At the age of 9 he accompanied his mother to Madinah.
2. Between the age of 9 and 12, he accompanied his uncle Abu-Talib on a business trip to Syria.
3. At the age of 25 he led Khadija's Caravan to Syria.

It is foolhardy to assume that the writing of the complete *Qur'an* resulted from the occasional chats and meetings with the Christians or Jews from any of the above three trips.

Logical grounds to prove that the Prophet did not learn the *Qur'an* from the Jews or Christians

The day-to-day life of the Prophet was an open book for all to see. In fact a revelation came asking people to give the Prophet privacy in his own home. If the Prophet had been meeting people who told him what to say as a revelation from God, this would not have been hidden for very long.

The extremely prominent nobles of the Quraish tribe, who followed the Prophet and subsequently accepted Islam, were wise and intelligent men who would have easily noticed anything suspicious about the way in which the Prophet brought the revelations to them - more so since the Prophetic mission lasted 23 years.

The enemies of the Prophet kept a close watch on him in order to find proof for their claim that he was a liar - they could not point out even a single instance when the Prophet may have had a secret rendezvous with particular Jews and Christians.

It is inconceivable that any human author of the *Qur'an* would have accepted a situation in which he received no credit whatsoever for originating the *Qur'an*.

Thus, historically and logically it cannot be established that there was a human source for the Qur'an.

The greatest proof that the Qur'an was not copied; Muhammad was an unlettered man

The theory that Muhammad authored the Qur'an or copied from other sources can be disproved by the single historical fact that he couldn't read or write.

God testifies Himself in the Qur'an,

"And you were not (able) to recite a Book before this (Book, the Qur'an came), nor were you (able) to transcribe it with your right hand: in that case, indeed, would the talkers of vanities have doubted." [114] God knew that many would doubt the authenticity of the Qur'an and would ascribe it to Prophet Muhammad. Therefore God in His Divine Wisdom chose the last and final Messenger to be an 'Ummi', i.e. unlettered, so that anyone who wanted to make any unfounded accusation would not then have the slightest justification to malign the Prophet. The accusation of his enemies that he had copied the Qur'an from other sources and rehashed it all in a beautiful language might have carried some

---

[114] The Holy Qur'an, Chapter 29, Verse 48

weight, but even this flimsy pretense has been deprived to the unbeliever and the cynic.

God reconfirms in the *Qur'an* in Surah Al A'raf chapter 7, verse 157:

"Those who follow the Messenger, the unlettered Prophet, whom they find mentioned in their own (Scriptures) in the Law and the Gospel"[115]

The prophecy of coming of the unlettered Prophet is also mentioned in the Bible in the book of Isaiah Chapter 29, Verse 12.

"And the book is delivered to him that is not learned, saying, Read this, I pray you: and he said, I am not learned."[116]

The *Qur'an* testifies in no less than four different places that the Prophet couldn't read or write.

Arabic version of the Bible was not even present, so how could it have been copied?

The Arabic version of the Bible had not been written at the time of Prophet Muhammad. The earliest Arabic version of the Old Testament is that of R. Saadias Gaon of 900 C.E. - more than 250 years after the death of our beloved Prophet. The oldest

---

[115] The Holy Qur'an, Chapter 7, Verse 157
[116] American King James Bible, Isaiah 29:12

Arabic version of the New Testament was published by Erpenius in 1616 C.E. - about a thousand years after the demise of our Prophet.

The actual reason for similarities in the *Qur'an* and the Bible; they are from a common source.

Any similarities that exist between the *Qur'an* and the Bible do not necessarily mean that the former has been copied from the latter. In fact it gives evidence that both of them are based on a common source; all divine revelations came from the same source – the one universal God. No matter what human changes were introduced into some of these Judeo-Christian and other older religious scriptures that had distorted their originality, there are some areas that have remained free from distortion and thus are common to the three Abrahamic religions.

It is true that there are some similar parallels between the *Qur'an* and the Bible but this is not sufficient to accuse Muhammad of compiling or copying from the Bible. The same logic would then also be applicable to teachings of Christianity and Judaism and thus one could wrongly claim that Jesus was not a genuine Prophet (God forbid) and that he simply copied from the Old Testament.

The similarities between the two signify a common source that is one true God and the continuation of the basic message of monotheism and not that the later prophets have plagiarized from the previous prophets.

If someone copies during an examination he will surely not write in the answer sheet that he has copied from his neighbor. Both the Qur'an and Prophet Muhammad gave due respect and credit to all the previous Prophets and the books that they brought, saying that the Qur'an testifies to the truth of the previous scriptures.

Muslims believe in the original Taurah, Zaboor, Injeel and Qur'an

Four revelations of God are mentioned by name in the Qur'an: the Taurah, the Zaboor, the Injeel and the Qur'an.

Taurah, which was the Revelation given to Moosa i.e. Moses.
Zaboor, which was the Revelation given to Dawood i.e. David.
Injeel, which was the Revelation given to Isa i.e. Jesus.
'Al-Qur'an , which was the last and final Revelation given to the last and final Messenger Muhammad.

It is an article of faith for every Muslim to believe in all the Prophets of God and all revelations of God. If a Muslim rejects any one of the Prophets or revelations, he is not regarded as a Muslim, because all books and prophets and messengers were sent from God, and so to disbelieve in one, is like disbelieving in them all

So a Muslim has to believe in the original scriptures to be a Muslim. However, the present day Bible has the first five books of the Old Testament attributed to Moses and the Psalms attributed to David.

Moreover, the Old Testament or the four Gospels of the New Testament are not the original *Taurah*, the *Zaboor* the *Injeel*, which the *Qur'an* refers to. These books of the present day Bible may partly contain the word of God but these books are certainly not the exact, accurate and complete revelations given to their respective prophets.

The *Qur'an* presents all the different prophets of God as belonging to one single brotherhood; all had a similar prophetic mission and the same basic message. Because of this, the fundamental teachings of the major faiths cannot be contradictory, even if there has been a considerable passage of time between the different prophetic missions, because the source of these missions was one: Almighty God. This is why the *Qur'an* says that the differences which exist between various religions are not the responsibility of the prophets, but of the followers of these prophets who forgot part of what they had been taught, and furthermore, misinterpreted and changed the scriptures. The *Qur'an* cannot therefore be seen as a scripture which competes with the teachings of Moses, Jesus and the other prophets. On the contrary, it confirms, completes and perfects the original messages that they actually brought to their people.

Another name for the *Qur'an* is the 'The *Furqan*' which means the criteria to judge the right from the wrong, and it is on the basis of the *Qur'an* that we can decipher which part of the previous scriptures can be considered to be the word of God. In other words, Muslims use the *Qur'an* as a yardstick to measure the accuracy of today's various Bibles. If the words agree with what the *Qur'an* says, it is likely to be original scripture. If it contradicts what the *Qur'an* says, then it cannot be from God. If it neither agrees nor disagrees, then we cannot pass judgment on it. It may be from the original scripture, it may not be.

There were many versions of the *Qur'an* all of which were burnt by Uthman, the third Caliph, except for one copy. Therefore is it not true that the present *Qur'an* is the one compiled by Uthman and not the original revelation of God?

I have touched upon this subject in another section of the book. One of the most common myths about the *Qur'an*, is that Uthman, the third Caliph of Islam authenticated and compiled one *Qur'an*, from a large set of mutually contradicting copies. The *Qur'an*, revered as the Word of God by Muslims the world over, is the same *Qur'an* as the one revealed to Prophet Muhammad. It was authenticated and written under his personal supervision. We will examine the roots of the myth, which says that Uthman had the *Qur'an* authenticated.

1. Prophet Muhammad himself supervised and authenticated the written texts of the *Qur'an*

Whenever the Prophet received a revelation, he would first memorize it himself and later let people know about the revelation and instruct his Companions, who would also memorize it. The Prophet would immediately ask the scribes to write down the revelation he had received, and he would reconfirm and re-check it himself. Prophet Muhammad was an unlettered person who could not read and write. Therefore, after receiving each revelation, he would repeat it to his Companions. They would write down the revelation, and he would re-check by asking them to read what they had written. If there was any mistake, the Prophet would immediately point it out and have it corrected and re-checked. Similarly he would even re-check and authenticate the portions of the *Qur'an* memorized by the Companions. In this way, the complete *Qur'an* was written down under the personal supervision of the prophet.

2. Order and sequence of *Qur'an* divinely inspired

The complete *Qur'an* was revealed over a period of 23 years portion by portion, as and when it was required. The *Qur'an* was not compiled by the Prophet in the chronological order of revelation. The order and sequence of the *Qur'an* too was divinely inspired and was instructed to the Prophet by God through Archangel Gabriel. Whenever a revelation was conveyed to his companions, the Prophet would also mention in which chapter and after which verse this new revelation should fit.

Every Ramadan, all the portions of the *Qur'an* that had been revealed, including the order of the verses, were revised and reconfirmed by the Prophet with Archangel Gabriel. During the last Ramadan, before the passing away of the Prophet, the *Qur'an* was re-checked and reconfirmed twice.

It is therefore clearly evident that the *Qur'an* was compiled and authenticated by the Prophet himself during his lifetime, both in the written form as well as in the memory of several of his Companions.

3. *Qur'an* copied on one common material

The complete *Qur'an*, along with the correct sequence of the verses, was present during the time of the Prophet. The verses however, were written on separate pieces, scraps of leather, thin flat stones, leaflets, palm branches, shoulder blades, etc. After the demise of the Prophet, Abu Bakr, the first caliph of Islam ordered that the *Qur'an* be copied from the various different materials on to a common material and place, which was in the shape of sheets. These were tied with strings so that nothing of the compilation was lost.

4. Uthman made copies of the Qur'an from the original manuscript

Many Companions of the Prophet used to write down the revelation of the Qur'an on their own whenever they heard it from the lips of the Prophet. All the verses revealed to the Prophet may not have been heard personally by all the Companions. There were high possibilities of different portions of the Qur'an being missed by different Companions. This gave rise to disputes among Muslims regarding the different contents of the Qur'an during the period of the third Caliph Uthman .

Uthman borrowed the original manuscript of the Qur'an, which was authorized by the beloved Prophet, from Hafsah (may God be pleased with her), the Prophet's wife. Uthman ordered four Companions who were among the scribes who wrote the Qur'an when the Prophet dictated it, led by Zaid bin Thabit to rewrite the script in several perfect copies. These were sent by Uthman to the main centers of Muslims.

There were other personal collections of the portions of the Qur'an that people had with them. These might have been incomplete and with mistakes. Uthman only appealed to the people to destroy all these copies, which did not match the original manuscript of the *Qur'an* in order to preserve the original text of the *Qur'an*. Two such copies of the copied text of the original *Qur'an* authenticated by the Prophet are present to this day, one at the museum in Tashkent in erstwhile Soviet Union and the other at the Topkapi Museum in Istanbul, Turkey.

5. Diacritical marks were added for non-Arabs

The original manuscript of the *Qur'an* does not have the signs indicating the vowels in Arabic script. These vowels are known as tashkil, zabar, zair, paish in Urdu and as fatah, damma and kasra in Arabic. The Arabs did not require the vowel signs and diacritical marks for correct pronunciation of the *Qur'an* since it was their mother tongue. For Muslims of non-Arab origin, however, it was difficult to recite the *Qur'an* correctly without the vowels. These marks were introduced into the *Qur'anic* script during the time of the fifth 'Umayyad' Caliph, Malik-ar-Marwan (66-86 Hijri/685-705 C.E.) and during the governorship of Al-Hajaj in Iraq.

Some people argue that the present copy of the *Qur'an* that we have along with the vowels and the diacritical marks is not the same original *Qur'an* that was present at the Prophet's time. But they fail to realize that the word 'Qur'an' means a recitation. Therefore, the preservation of the recitation of the *Qur'an* is important, irrespective of whether the script is different or whether it contains vowels. If the pronunciation and the Arabic is the same, naturally, the meaning remains the same too.

6. God Himself has promised to guard the *Qur'an*

God has promised in the Qur'an: "We have, without doubt, sent down the Message; and We will assuredly Guard it (from corruption)." [117]

---

[117] The Holy *Qur'an*, Chapter 15, Verse 9

"Muslims aided the Nazis in World War II against the Jewish People"

This is one of the most horrific accusations against the Muslims. This is based upon the allegations that the Grand Mufti of Jerusalem colluded with Hitler during the Second World War to exterminate Jews. There are also allegations that during post-war trials against the Nazis, the Mufti's name was mentioned in testimony alleging his support of the Nazis.

The aforementioned Pamela Geller mentions in an article:

"During the Nuremberg Trials in July 1946, Eichmann's assistant, Dieter Wisliczeny, testified that Mufti was a central figure in the planning of the genocide of the Jews:

"The Grand Mufti has repeatedly suggested to the Nazi authorities – including Hitler, von Ribbentrop and Himmler – the extermination of European Jewry. ... The Mufti was one of the initiators of the systematic extermination of European Jewry and had been a collaborator and adviser of Eichmann and Himmler in the execution of this plan... He was one of Eichmann's best friends and had constantly incited him to accelerate the extermination measures. I heard him say, accompanied by Eichmann, he had visited incognito the gas chambers of Auschwitz."

Wisliczeny also testified that al-Husseini asked Heinrich Himmler to send one of Eichmann's assistants to Jerusalem once the war was over, to aid the Mufti in "solving the Jewish question in the Middle East."[118]

However, court transcripts of the Nuremberg trials show no mention of the Mufti in Wisliczeny's testimony.[119]

A more rational explanation for the work of this man was that he was an Arab National. Initially he was against the British occupation of Palestine, and he fought against this occupation, leading to his subsequent arrest and exile. When the British gave amnesty to all exiled nationals, he returned and found that the Zionist movement was gaining momentum, and he fought against that movement to try to protect Palestine. There are even records of him addressing the local Jews, who had resided there for centuries, telling them that he had no enmity towards them. The big issue that he had was with the loss of Palestinian land in an unjust land-grab.

In any case, even if the allegations against him are true, the evil work of one man should not overshadow the hundreds of thousands of Muslim lives lost fighting for the Allied armies *against* Nazi forces.

---

[118] http://bigjournalism.com/p-eller/2010/02/07/the-mufti-of-jerusalem-architect-of-the-holocaust/
[119] http://avalon.law.yale.edu/imt/01-03-46.asp#wisliceny

In the summer of 2010, I had the opportunity to visit Paris. In addition to the usual tourist attractions and landmarks, I heard about a beautiful mosque in one of the suburbs of Paris. I decided to pay it a visit. When I got there, I found that the mosque's history was extremely fascinating. It had been built by the French government to honor the Muslim forces that fought alongside the French in World War I. The history of the beautiful mosque doesn't stop there. During World War II, the Imam of the mosque was well-known to have distributed falsified certificates to Jews to fool the Nazi forces into thinking that they were Muslims.

The person behind this rescue effort was the director of the mosque, whose name was Si Kaddour Benghabrit. This little known fact of history has been documented in a book, *The Grand Mosque of Paris: A Story of How Muslims Rescued JewsDuring the Holocaust* by Karen Gray Ruelle and Deborah Durland Desaix.[120] According to this book, the Jews as well as downed Allied forces were sheltered in the mosque until they could escape safely. The story of this heroism has also been turned into a movie called *"Les Hommes Libres" ("Free Men")*. [121]

---

[120] *The Grand Mosque of Paris: A Story of How Muslims Rescued Jews During the Holocaust* by Karen Gray Ruelle and Deborah Durland Desaix ISBN 978-0823421596

[121] http://www.nytimes.com/2011/10/04/movies/how-a-paris-mosque-sheltered-jews-in-the-holocaust.html?pagewanted=all

Another book, *Among the Righteous: Lost Stories from the Holocaust's Long Reach into Arab Lands* by Robert Satloff, Executive Director of The Washington Institute for Near East Policy, documents how Arabs in North African Muslim countries helped protect persecuted Jews from the Holocaust.

Also, an award-winning movie, *Days of Glory,* has been made to honor the North African Muslim soldiers that died fighting alongside the Allied forces in World War II. The original name of the movie was *Indigènes*, French for "The Indigenous" or "The Natives", referring to the local North Africans who took it upon themselves to fight for a noble cause.[122]

Amongst Albanian Muslims, a code of honor called *Besa* compelled them to take in and shelter Jews during the Holocaust. Countless stories exist about these unsung Muslim heroes. It is said that even Jews who came across the borders from other countries were helped and protected under the code of honor.

The remarkable assistance afforded to the Jews was grounded in *Besa*, a code of honor, which still today serves as the highest ethical code in the country. *Besa*, means literally "to keep the promise." One who acts according to *Besa* is someone who keeps his word, someone to whom one can trust one's life and the

---

[122] http://en.wikipedia.org/wiki/Days_of_Glory_(2006_film) and http://www.imdb.com/title/tt0444182/

lives of one's family. **Apparently this code sprouted from the Muslim faith as interpreted by the Albanians.**

The help afforded to Jews and non-Jews alike should be understood as a matter of national honor. The Albanians went out of their way to provide assistance; moreover, they competed with each other for the privilege of saving Jews. These acts originated from compassion, loving kindness and a desire to help those that were in need, even those of another faith or origin. This was solely due to the *Besa* code of honor rooted in Islamic teachings.

According to a website dedicated to honor people that helped Holocaust victims:

"Following the German occupation in 1943, the Albanian population, in an extraordinary act, refused to comply with the occupier's orders to turn over lists of Jews residing within the country's borders. Moreover, the various governmental agencies provided many Jewish families with fake documentation that allowed them to intermingle amongst the rest of the population. The Albanians not only protected their Jewish citizens, but also provided sanctuary to Jewish refugees who had arrived in Albania, when Albania, the only European country with a Muslim majority, succeeded in the place where other European nations failed. Almost all Jews living within Albanian borders during the German occupation, those of Albanian origin and refugees alike, were saved, except members of a single family. **Impressively, there were more Jews in Albania at the end of the war than beforehand.**"[123]

Turning to Britain, there is a fascinating story of a Muslim lady who descended from royalty, and resided in England. Her name was Noor Inayat Khan, and she worked behind enemy lines as the first female wireless operator to be sent to France in World War II. She descended from Tipu Sultan, the famous 18th century ruler of the Kingdom of Mysore. Her story was told in a BBC program, and can be found on Youtube[124]. When you hear about her heroics, you have to remind yourself that what you are hearing is not a fictional spy novel, but something that actually happened; she was an actual person, and the events mentioned in her life actually occurred. The most important point that can be impressed upon the readers of this book is that she was a Muslim, and her pacifist beliefs compelled her to venture behind enemy lines completely unarmed. She refused to carry a gun. She met a tragic end, ending up being shot to death in a concentration camp. She was awarded the highest medals for bravery. She was posthumously Mentioned in Despatches (MID, a name for a military award), awarded a British George Cross, appointed a Member of the Order of the British Empire and awarded a French Croix de Guerre with Gold Star. Khan was the third of three Second World War FANY

123

http://www1.yadvashem.org/yv/en/exhibitions/besa/introduction.asp
[124]http://www.youtube.com/watch?v=2FxkU9ZcVc8&feature=context
&context=C38b8f86UDOEgsToPDskJCVqo7Ri0E6_2BtPm-bmO_

(First Aid Nursing Yeomanry) members to be awarded the George Cross, Britain's highest award for gallantry not on the battle field. At the beginning of 2011, a campaign was launched to raise £100,000 for a bronze bust of her in central London close to her former home.[12] It has been reported that this will be the first memorial in Britain to either a Muslim or an Asian woman,[13] although she is already commemorated on the FANY memorial in St Paul's Church, Wilton Place, Knightsbridge, London,[14] which lists the 54 members of the Corps who gave their lives on active service.

Her exploits have been written in a book; *Spy Princess: A life of Noor Inayat Khan.*[125] by Shrabani Basu. There is a detailed account of her life found on many websites.[126]

The partition of India into two countries took place in 1947. Prior to that time, India was under colonial rule by the British. According to statistics, at the outbreak of the Second World War, the Indian army numbered 205,000 men. Later on during the Second World War the Indian Army would become the largest all-volunteer force in history, rising to over 2.5 million men in size. Undoubtedly, many of these soldiers would have been Muslims, as the population of India was made up of a large

[125] Basu, Shrabani. *Spy Princess: The Life of Noor Inayat Khan",* Sutton Publishing, 2006
[126] http://en.wikipedia.org/wiki/Noor_Inayat_Khan

proportion of Muslims, much like it is today. 87,000 Indian soldiers lost their lives in this war. [127]

Many Indians were awarded medals for their bravery in the Second World War. As many as 30 Victoria crosses were awarded to Indian soldiers.[128]

If you visit the website for the Commonwealth War Graves Commission[129], which lists the lives lost by British Commonwealth forces, and put in the search engine the name "Mohammed", the search engine responds "there are too many results, the first 1001 are displayed". Bear in mind that the name Muhammad is a common name for Muslims, but it is not the only name. I tested the search engine using my last name "Sheikh", and it gave the same result; "there are too many results, the first 1001 are displayed". Just imagine if you could list all of the Muslim names that gave the ultimate sacrifice to fight the tyrant Adolf Hitler.

The above examples and statistics put to rest the fallacy of those who claim that Muslims colluded with Adolf Hitler in World War II, and bring to light the forgotten heroes of the Muslim world that fought for justice during the Second World War..

---

[127] http://en.wikipedia.org/wiki/British_Indian_Army
[128]http://en.wikipedia.org/wiki/List_of_Indian_Victoria_Cross_recipients
[129] http://www.cwgc.org

Kareem Rashad Sultan Khan was one of the many Muslim soldiers that lost their lives in the wars following the terrorist attacks.

According to the Gannett News Service, he was "spurred by the September 11 attacks on the World Trade Center [and] wanted to show that not all Muslims were fanatics and that many, like him, were willing to lay their lives down for their country, America. He enlisted immediately after graduation and was sent to Iraq in July 2006." He was promoted posthumously to the rank of Corporal, and received a Bronze Star and a Purple Heart for his honorable service.

His service was cited during a 19 October 2008 interview on Meet the Press with General Colin Powell. In particular, Powell referred to a photograph in The New Yorker which showed Khan's mother by his gravestone in Arlington National Cemetery. Powell said Khan's example refutes the anti-Muslim sentiment present in the Republican campaign during the 2008 U.S. Presidential election, namely that being Muslim disqualifies a person from being a genuine, patriotic American, or that a Muslim could not become President.[130]

"Muslims are supposed to kill Jews and Christians"

Another variant to the above mentioned misconception is that Muslims "are supposed to kill all non-believers".

Again, we must turn to logic, in this case historical proof, that this is simply not true.

Muslims ruled over Spain for over 700 years. Yet at the end of their rule, they were expelled by none other than the Christian Queen Isabella. This expulsion, which also severely victimized the Jews that had also been thriving under Islamic rule, was known historically as the Spanish Inquisition. If we think with an open mind, 700 years would have been quite sufficient to exterminate all non-Muslims, but it didn't happen.

Let's look at another example. Muslims ruled Palestine for over 1300 years. During these 1300 years, Jews and Christians were free to worship and live in Palestine without any hindrance. All of the holy sites, the synagogues, the churches, the birthplace of Jesus, the places of Jesus' miracles, were all meticulously preserved and protected during Islamic rule. Again, 1300 years was ample time to exterminate all other religions, but it just didn't happen.

According to Islamic historians, when Muslims entered Jerusalem under the leadership of the Caliph Umar ibn Al-Khattab, a pact was agreed at the Church of the Holy Sepulcher, the reputed birthplace of Christ. The wording of the pact is a clear reflection of religious freedom allowed in the City.

Here is the wording of that pact:

"In the Name of Allah, the Most Merciful, the Most Compassionate

This is an assurance of peace and protection given by the servant of Allah Omar, Commander of the Believers to the people of Ilia' (Jerusalem). He gave them an assurance of protection for their lives, property, church and crosses as well as the sick and healthy and all its religious community.

Their churches shall not be occupied, demolished nor taken away wholly or in part. None of their crosses or property shall be seized. They shall not be coerced in their religion nor shall any of them be injured. None of the Jews shall reside with them in Ilia'.

The people of Ilia shall pay Jizia tax (tax on free non-Muslims living under Muslim rule) as inhabitants of cities do. They shall evict all Romans and thieves.

He whoever gets out shall be guaranteed safety for his life and property until he reaches his safe haven. He whoever stays shall be (also) safe, in which case he shall pay as much tax as the people of Ilia' do. Should any of the people of Ilia wish to move together with his property along with the Romans and to clear out of their churches and crosses, they shall be safe for their lives, churches and crosses, until they have reached their safe haven. He whoever chooses to stay he may do so and he shall pay as much tax as the people of Ilia' do. He whoever wishes to move along with the Roman, may do so, and whoever wishes to return back home to his kinsfolk, may do so. Nothing shall be taken from them, their crops have been harvested. To the contents of this convent here are given the Covenant of Allah, the guarantees of His Messenger, the Caliphs and the Believers, provided they (the people of Ilia') pay their due Jizia tax.

Khalid Ibn al-Waleed Amr Ibn al-Ass Abdul-Rahman Ibn'Auf Mu'awiya Ibn abi-Sifian Made and executed in the year 15 AH."[131]

This pact has been mentioned by renowned Islamic historians such as Tabari, although the wording is disputed. However, upon observation, the fair treatment of Jews and Christians in Palestine throughout the ages under Islamic rule is in accordance with the above agreement, with freedom for all faiths to practice freely.

Readers should be aware of another version "Pact of Umar" that has been publicized by Islamophobes as the actual Pact. The summary of that so-called Pact was that the Christians wrote to Umar with some stringent conditions that they imposed upon themselves, Umar agreed with those conditions, and that became the "Pact of Umar".

---

[131] Tabari, Tarikh At-Tabari, Vol. 3, p.609

However, Muslim scholars have regarded this second so-called Pact as a forgery, with no historical authenticity.

According to Maher Abu-Munshar, author of *Islamic Jerusalem And Its Christians: A History of Tolerance And Tensions*:

"The humiliating conditions enumerated in the so-called "Pact of Umar" are utterly foreign to the mentality, thoughts and practices of this caliph...The deficiencies [in the textual integrity] support the contention that Umar was not the originator of the document. In addition to the remarkable care and concern displayed in Umar's attitude to dhimmis confirms the rejection of the so-called Pact of Umar as attributable to Caliph Umar Ibn al-Khattab. The Pact of Umar was not the work of Umar Ibn al-Khattab."[132]

In *Sahih-al-Bukhari,* a renowned collection of the sayings of the Prophet regarded as authentic by Muslims, Imam Bukhari writes a chapter entitled, "One should fight for the protection of the ahl al-dhimma and they should not be enslaved."

Under this heading, Bukhari narrates the following instructions on the authority of Umar ibn al-Khattab, when he was stabbed and dying of the wound inflicted upon him by a Persian slave: "I strongly recommend him [the next caliph] to take care of those non-Muslims who are under God and His Prophet's protection in that he should remain faithful to them according

---

[132] Maher Abu-Munshar, Islamic Jerusalem And Its Christians: A History of Tolerance And Tensions, pp.79-80

to the covenant with them, and fight on their behalf and not burden them [by imposing high taxes] beyond their capacity."

When one reads these instructions, left by the dying caliph as the head of Muslim state to honor the sacred covenant offered by God and his emissary to the people of the Book, the Jews and the Christians, it is hard to believe that the Pact of Umar ascribed to the second caliph could be regarded as authentic.

Even Western historians agree. Abraham P. Bloch says:

"Omar ibn al-Khattab (634-644), the second caliph, conquered Palestine, Syria, Iraq, Persia, and Egypt. Jews and Christians were permitted to continue their communal existence. Omar was a tolerant ruler, unlikely to impose humiliating conditions upon non-Muslims, or to infringe upon their religious and social freedoms. His name has been erroneously associated...with the restrictive Covenant of Omar."[133]

To summarize, Islam doesn't order us to hate Jews and Christians. The verses of the *Qur'an* that are purported to be understood in such a way have a completely different meaning than the one portrayed.

---

[133] Abraham P. Bloch, One a Day: An Anthology of Jewish Historical Anniversaries for Every Day of the Year, p.314

"Muslims are not supposed to befriend Jews and Christians"

This misunderstanding is based upon a verse of the *Qur'an* that is often quoted out of context. Here is that verse:

"O you who believe, do not take the Jews and the Christians for intimate friends. They are friends to each other. Whoever takes them as intimate friends is one of them. Surely, Allah does not take the unjust people to the right path."

On the face of it, this verse seems very clear in prohibiting people from befriending Jews and Christians. However, the real meaning is revealed in the very next verses:

"Now, you see those who have disease in their hearts race towards them saying, "We apprehend that some misfortune may overtake us." So, it is likely that Allah may bring victory or something else from His own side, whereupon they will become regretful over what they concealed in their hearts. Those who believe will say, "Are these the ones who swore their solemn oaths by Allah that they were with you?" Their deeds have gone to waste, and they became losers."[134]

The background to these verses was that the hypocrites, who openly proclaimed faith, but internally they disbelieved, were always afraid that they would get caught, and then they would

---

[134] The Holy Quran, Chapter 5, Verses 51-53.

get into trouble with the Muslims. They are described in the second verse as "those that have a disease in their hearts".

To prepare themselves for this inevitable course of events, they approached the Jews and Christians in Madinah, and requested them to become allied with them *against* the Muslims, to fight against them.

So this ruling is not a general ruling for everyone. Rather, it is a ruling for those people that want to fight against the Muslims by allying themselves with other non-Muslims.

Thinking logically, if Muslims were not supposed to befriend Jews and Christians, why are Muslim men allowed to marry Jewish and Christian women? Marriage is something way beyond simple friendship, so if marriage is allowed, certainly friendship should be allowed. It's something that needs to be considered before making false assumptions based on hearsay.

"Academic Reports"

In the last few years, there has been a surge in "academic think tanks" that release reports from time to time.

These reports are labeled "academic reports", but they are not written independently and objectively. When one reads these reports, it is very apparent that the purpose behind the reports is simply to malign Islam and Muslims, and to make sure that innocent Muslims remain under public scrutiny for being "potential terrorists" or "sleeper cells" ready to carry out operations against the United States at a moment's notice.

The most alarming result of such reports is that because of their very official-looking and seemingly academic nature, people are actually fooled into believing that they are accurate. If only people scratched a little below the surface, they would realize that there is no legitimacy to the purported threats highlighted in these papers.

The following are examples of such reports.

Islam in America's Classrooms; History or Propaganda?

Islam in America's Classrooms History or Propaganda is written by the group Act for America, an anti-Islamic hate group that is headed by the aforementioned Brigitte Gabriel. The report is targeting publishers of school textbooks, who according to their estimation are portraying Islam in a positive light, and therefore brainwashing "vulnerable" children.

A section from this apparently damning report reads:

"There are two primary strategies for subjugating non-believers. Violent jihad includes wars of conquest and world-wide terror campaigns to intimidate and eventually subjugate infidels. Islamic terrorists are constantly in the news for their horrible acts. They are willing to use any means available to them—including weapons of mass destruction and child suicide bombers—to achieve their goals. Cultural or stealth jihad includes infiltration, propaganda, "lawfare" and playing the victim when they are actually the aggressor. Moderate Islamists wage stealth jihad through patient advocacy of their ideology, incremental social change, lawsuits, immigration, high fertility rates, intimidation of opponents and sophisticated propaganda. Violent and stealth jihadists have the same goal, world domination. They use different strategies and tactics that complement each other."

It's quite amusing to read that Muslims have "high fertility rates". As if it's a matter of choice whether you are fertile, infertile, or highly fertile!

The basic gist of the report is the same as mentioned before in the chapter entitled *Shariah Law is Taking Over the Country*; the preposterous claim that Muslims are slowly but surely infiltrating into American society using "stealth tactics", and before we know it the whole country will be subjugated by Muslim rulers.

Shariah; The Threat to America

Another report, written by Frank Gaffney's Center for Security Policy, is ominously titled *Shariah; The Threat to America.* In this report, the threat is outlined as The Muslim Brotherhood, an Egyptian organization that apparently has designs on taking over the world. The summary of the whole report is based around this threat.

However when you actually read the report, you will discover that the whole threat is based on a mundane document which the report calls *Explanatory Memorandum,* apparently written by an obscure man named Mohamed Akram, which the report claims was "a senior Hamas leader in the United States". I have tried to search for this man online using various search terms, and have yet to find out who he is. All I can find is the same regurgitated claim, that Mohamed Akram wrote this Memorandum, with no available clue as to his identity.

Let's face it; if this man was such a big fish in Hamas, or as the report claims "a senior Hamas leader", shouldn't we know something about him? Most of the anti-Islamic rhetoric we find in this report is based on this single banal claim that a guy called Akram wrote a document highlighting his agenda for America, and we don't even know who the author really is!

The report then ties in virtually *all* prominent American Islamic organizations to this document, claiming that all these organizations are all subsidiaries of the Muslim Brotherhood, and are all hell-bent on fulfilling the purported agenda in the document. There is no proof offered as to how the organizations are connected to the Muslim Brotherhood. It seems that merely by virtue of being an Islamic organization, you become part of the Muslim Brotherhood.

To summarize, blanket accusations are made against Muslims and Islamic organizations based on a vague document. But if the "document" has no authenticity, or no means of verification, the whole accusation can be assumed to be little more than a conspiracy theory.

One of the biggest Islamic organizations that come under scrutiny in this report is the Islamic Society of North America, better known as ISNA. The unsubstantiated claim is made that ISNA is a front for the Muslim Brotherhood, based on information found in the aforementioned purported "document". However, many prominent politicians on both sides of the political spectrum have supported ISNA, and they seem oblivious to the asserted threat posed by ISNA. Scores of public figures have spoken at ISNA conferences, including White House advisor Karen Hughes, Congressman Henry Hyde,

Congressman Bob Barr, Congressman David Bonior, Congressman Tom Campbell, Congresswoman Marcy Kaptur, White House advisor Valerie Jarrett, officers of the U.S. Military, rabbis, priests, pastors (including conservative pastor and best-selling author Rick Warren), and letters of support have been sent from Presidents Clinton, George W. Bush, and Barack Obama.

Other methods adopted in this report are misquoting, explaining out of context, and misrepresenting verses from the *Qur'an* and sayings of the Prophet Muhammad, thereby showing that the whole of the holy book of Muslims is littered with verses of violence. Most of those verses, if not all, will be explained later in this book, with detailed explanations about their true meaning.

Shariah and Violence in American Mosques

This study is the most amusing from all of the reports that I have read. It is written by Mordechai Kedar and David Yerushalmi. Yerushalmi is the anti-Islamic lawyer behind writing anti-*Shariah* legislation in many states.

Here is a section from the report. I will put in bold letters the sections that I want to turn your attention to:

"Potential recruits who are swept up in this movement may find their inspiration and encouragement in a place with ready access to classic and modern literature that is positive toward jihad and violence,

where highly Sharia adherent behavior is practiced, and where a society exists that in some form promotes a culture of martyrdom or at least engages in activities that are supportive of violent jihad. **The mosque can be such a place. That the mosque is a societal apparatus that might serve as a support mechanism for violent jihad may seem self-evident, but for it to be a useful means for measuring radicalization requires empirical evidence.** *A 2007 study by the New York city police department noted that, in the context of the mosque, high levels of Sharia adherence, termed "Salafi ideology" by the authors of the report, may relate to support for violent jihad. Specifically, it found that highly Sharia-adherent mosques have played a prominent role in radicalization.7* **Another study found a relationship between frequency of mosque attendance and a predilection for supporting suicide attacks but discovered no empirical evidence linking support for suicide bombings to some measure of religious devotion (defined and measured by frequency of prayer).8 However, the study suffers from a major methodological flaw, namely, reliance on self-reporting of prayer frequency.** *Muslims would be under social and psychological pressure to report greater prayer frequency because their status as good or pious believers is linked to whether they fulfill the religious obligation to pray five times a day. This piety is not dependent on regular mosque attendance as Muslims are permitted to pray outside of a mosque environment whenever necessary."*

In this small section, the following should be noted:

1. The authors have come to an automatic conclusion that the mosque is the place that is supportive of violent jihad. Not only do they conclude that it *is* the case, they say it is "self-evident". But what does that mean? Self-evident based on what? Isn't evidence needed to prove that's the case?

2. A study that concluded that devotion to prayer rituals doesn't necessarily equate to radicalization has been declared by this report as being flawed. What is the flaw? Nothing scientific, no statistical evidence. Just the *possibility* that people, due to psychological pressure be forced to misrepresent how many times they are praying in the mosque. The bottom line is that any study that doesn't prove their agenda is "flawed".

This is taken from the first few paragraphs. If you continue to read this report, it becomes more and more strange.

The writers of the report came to a conclusion that the combination of the following three things determined whether someone is radical or not:

1. *Shariah* adherence (in other words simply practicing Islam)

2. Islamic literature that "shows violence in a positive light"

3. "Institutional support" for violent jihad

"Surveyors" (i.e. spies) were sent into mosques and were told to watch for the following "*Shariah*-adherent practices". The report says:

"Among the behaviors observed at the mosques and scored as Sharia-adherent were: (a)women wearing the *hijab* (head covering) or *niqab* (full-length shift covering the entire female form except for the eyes); (b) gender segregation during mosque prayers; and (c) enforcement of straight prayer lines."

For the non-Muslim reading this report as an outsider, it might seem acceptable to assume that these are "radical" behaviors. But for the practicing Muslim, this is bread-and-butter, run-of-the-mill, everyday- practiced Islamic adherence to prayer. There is nothing radical or extreme about it. Further on in the report, "*Shariah*-adherent" behavior is described as the following:

1. The length of the Imam's beard, and whether it was dyed or not
2. Whether the Imam wore a head-covering or not
3. The clothing of the Imam
4. Whether the Imam wore the watch on his right wrist or not (right wrist=radical, left wrist=not radical. Needless to say this was the most amusing part of the report.)
5. Adult male worshippers' clothing
6. Adult female worshippers' clothing
7. Girls 5-12 wearing hijab

8. Boys 5-12 wearing head-covering

For comparison's sake, let's take the church rulings of the Roman Catholic Church. If you were to say that a celibate priest is a sign of the extreme nature of Catholic teachings. Or to say that the collar worn by a priest is extreme. These are normal practices of the Catholic Church, and don't hint at anything nefarious. Similar to this example is the portrayal of Muslims innocently practicing day-to-day mundane religious acts mentioned as "radical" in this ridiculous report.

The appearance of the Imam is important for the congregation, not for reasons of radicalism, but because of the position that he has in the community. His dress, his features, how he carries himself are all scrutinized *because* he is the leader of the community. Just imagine you are waiting at the airport, and pilot of the plane you are about to board comes in wearing a t-shirt and Bermuda shorts. The first thing that will come to your mind is, is this person taking his job seriously? You can use the same example for doctors, firemen, policemen etc. The uniform of a person signifies the character of that person. This is why the appearance of the Imam is important, and he is expected to live up to that high standard by the community. The wearing of robes, a head-covering etc. are all important aspects of that dress.

As for the beard, Muslims believe that all messengers sent by God had beards. Let's face it. Have you ever seen *any* image of Jesus without a beard?

One must question the objectivity of such reports that declare something that is so common in the Islamic community as equated with radicalism. It's just one step short of declaring, or even equivalent to declaring "All Muslims are radical extremists".

And the watch worn on the right wrist is a sign of radicalism? To put something so stupid in an alleged "academic study" belies belief! This claim alone shows that the study lacks objectivity, relies on weak information, and becomes material for late-night comedy shows. Are you reading this, Jon Stewart?

Can you imagine all the terrorists in the world, lurking in their caves, foaming at the mouth, declaring, "Curse those infidels! They have discovered how to uncover us terrorists just by looking at our watches! Now we must wear our watch on our left hands!" Realistically, there is no Islamic ruling that I know of related to which wrist the watch should be worn on.

To summarize; the equation of an imam's dress, watch and beard with radicalism is nonsensical to say the least.

As for the "literature that shows violence in a positive light", the following examples are given in the report:

1. *Tafsir ibn Kathir*

2. *Fiqh us-Sunnah*
3. *Riyadhussaliheen*
4. Books by Mawdudi
5. Books by Sayyid Qutb

The first three books are likely to be found in *every* mosque in the country. That is because they are foundational books on the subject they discuss.

Tafsir ibn Kathir is a commentary of the *Qur'an*. It explains verses of the *Qur'an* that have some ambiguity to them, and is accepted across the Muslim world as a source that a layperson can turn to when he or she needs an explanation of the *Qur'an*.

Riyadhussaliheen is a book that is a compilation of the sayings of the Prophet Muhammad. Again, it is accepted across the Muslim world as a book for the layperson to turn to when he wants to study a specific subject, and see what the Prophet has said about it, he turns to this book.

Fiqh us-Sunnah is a book of Islamic jurisprudence, which teaches the Muslim layperson about everyday issues, like purification of the body, how to pray, rules related to fasting etc. Again, it's a book that is a source for the layperson that has any question related to his everyday life.

If you look at the trend of the whole report, things that are in common practice amongst the Muslims is characterized as "extreme". The choice of these books by the report authors follows that trend, namely that every Muslim reads these books, so every Muslim must be extreme.

I suggest to every reader to go to the following websites and read the books yourself to see if they are truly radical.

Tafsir ibn Kathir can be found at
http://Qur'an.worldofislam.info/tafsir/index.htm

Riyadhussaliheen can be found at http://www.witness-pioneer.org/vil/hadeeth/riyad/

Fiqhussunah can be found at
http://abdurrahman.org/Sunnah/FiqhusSunnah/

Commentary of the *Qur'an* by Mawdudi can be found at http://www.englishtafseer.com

The other authors mentioned in the report, Mawdudi and Qutb, are not as commonly used as a reference by Muslims. However, any radical views that are portrayed in their writings maybe due to the environment in which they grew up in, or found themselves in. Both lived under colonial British rule, and saw the colonialist establishment living lavish lifestyles at the expense of the indigenous poor.

Sayyid Qutb's treatment by his government was even worse. He wrote his commentary *In the Shade of the Qur'an* while imprisoned. It goes without saying that one who is subjected to such harsh treatment will inevitably portray anti-establishment views in his writings, and that kind of stance is actually reflected in Qutb's works. He was eventually hung by the then pro-Communist Jamal Abdel Nasir for his staunch stance against the government and Communism.

"The Qur'an says that Jews are pigs and monkeys"

This is one of the most talked about issues when talking about the relationship between Jews and Muslims. The contention is that Muslims regard Jews as pigs and monkeys. The issue becomes negatively exacerbated when radical imams use this kind of twisted rhetoric in their speeches.

So what does the Qur'an say about Jews?

If you open the second chapter of the Qur'an, entitled The Cow, God addresses the Children of Israel in many verses. The gist of the conversation is that God reminds the Israelites of the blessings that he bestowed upon them again and again. Included in the list of those blessings was escape from the persecution of Pharaoh. I would encourage everyone to read this chapter and understand how God actually blessed the children of Israel.

So where did this story of pigs and monkeys come from?

There is a story in the Qur'an that talks about a specific Israelite village that disobeyed God in the strict rulings related to the Sabbath. God tested this village, which was on the edge of the sea, by sending plenty of fish on Saturdays, and very few fish on other days. But instead of respecting the Sabbath and refraining from fishing on Saturday, they twisted the command of God, and put out their nets on Fridays, and collected the fish on Sundays, claiming that they did not actually fish on Saturday.

Ultimately, when this disobedience continued, despite the prohibition from the village elders, God sent down a punishment to this village, and turned them into pigs and monkeys.

This story is not about all Jews; rather it is about a specific group of people in a village who disobeyed God. They were condemned to punishment not because of who they were, but for what they did, namely disobey God in the strict rules of the Sabbath. So to take this story, and twist it into a fabricated accusation is completely unethical according to all standards.

Why are these kinds of stories mentioned in the *Qur'an*? The reason is very simple. We are told stories of many previous nations who disobeyed when they were supposed to be obeying God and the messengers that he sent. We hear these stories, and we are advised that we should not make the same mistakes that these previous nations made. The purpose is not to use it as a tool for condemning any one group or individual, as certain people have chosen to do, but as a reminder that we must not make similar mistakes in our obedience to God.

"Muslims want to blow Israel off the map"

This sentence became famous when Ahmadinejad, the President of Iran, made a statement to this effect. According to him he was mistranslated, but that is beside the point. Most Muslims do not have this kind of philosophy. In fact, most would say that they are in favor of a two-state solution with Israel and Palestine living in peace and security with each other as neighbors.

One sentiment that Muslims do have however, is that in 1948, another country *was* blown off the map; this country was Palestine. The formation of Israel resulted in obliterating the whole of Palestine, leaving just two small pieces of land, the West Bank and the Gaza Strip, for the Palestinian Arabs Muslims and Christians that had lived there for over a millennium, with the exception of the years of the Crusades.

In fact, there is a whole industry dedicated to the denial of the very *existence* of Palestine prior to 1948, which adds insult to injury. The argument presented is that Palestine was a region which just *happened* to have Bedouin Arab tribes living there.[135]

The answer to this outrageous accusation is simple. All countries in the region have Arab tribes living in them. It doesn't automatically equate to Egypt, Jordan, Syria, Iraq,

---

[135] http://www.wnd.com/2002/03/13240/

Kuwait etc. etc. *not* being self-governed countries with their own names. Just as they have their own names, rulers, presidents and prime ministers, Palestine also was a country prior to Israel's formation.

Even as recently as the end of 2011, Newt Gingrich, presidential candidate for the Republican party, stated in an interview that the Palestinians were an "invented people".

He further said, "I think that we've had an invented Palestinian people who are in fact Arabs and who were historically part of the Arab community. And they had a chance to go many places, and for a variety of political reasons we have sustained this war against Israel now since the 1940s, and it's tragic."[136]

Golda Meir, Prime Minister of Israel from 1969 to 1974, had many quotes denying the existence of Palestine. Here are a few of them:

"There is no such thing as a Palestinian people... It is not as if we came and threw them out and took their country. They didn't exist."[137]

"How can we return the occupied territories? There is nobody to return them to."[138]

---

[136] http://www.guardian.co.uk/world/2011/dec/10/palestinians-invented-people-newt-gingrich
[137] Golda Meir, statement to The Sunday Times, 15 June, 1969.
[138] Golda Meir, March 8, 1969.

"Anyone who speaks in favor of bringing the Arab refugees back must also say how he expects to take the responsibility for it, if he is interested in the state of Israel. It is better that things are stated clearly and plainly: We shall not let this happen." [139]

"This country exists as the fulfillment of a promise made by God Himself. It would be ridiculous to ask it to account for its legitimacy."[140]

Moshe Dayan, Defense Minister and later Foreign Minister of Israel, was quoted by Edward Said:

"Jewish villages were built in the place of Arab villages. You do not even know the names of these Arab villages, and I do not blame you because geography books no longer exist. Not only do the books not exist, the Arab villages are not there either. Nahlal arose in the place of Mahlul; Kibbutz Gvat in the place of Jibta; Kibbutz Sarid in the place of Huneifis; and Kefar Yehushua in the place of Tal al-Shuman. There is not a single place built in this country that did not have a former Arab population."[141]

Noam Chomsky quotes in his book, *Fateful Triangle: The United States, Israel, and the Palestinians*, a saying of David Ben Gurion,

[139] Golda Meir, 1961, in a speech to the Knesset, reported in Ner, October 1961

[140] Golda Meir, Le Monde, 15 October 1971

[141] Edward Said, 'Zionism from the Standpoint of Its Victims', Social Text, Volume 1, 1979, 7-58

the first Prime Minister of Israel: "Let us not ignore the truth among ourselves ... politically we are the aggressors and they defend themselves... The country is theirs, because they inhabit it, whereas we want to come here and settle down, and in their view we want to take away from them their country."[142]

In fact, the Balfour Declaration, which officially introduced the idea of a Jewish State, has at its wording: "His Majesty's government view with favor the establishment *in Palestine* of a national home for the Jewish people, and will use their best endeavors to facilitate the achievement of this object, it being clearly understood that nothing shall be done which may prejudice the civil and religious rights of existing non-Jewish communities *in Palestine*, or the rights and political status enjoyed by Jews in any other country." (Emphasis added)

The wording clearly states that Palestine was already there, and the Jewish homeland would be *in Palestine*, without infringing upon the rights of the non-Jewish Palestinians that were already living there. We are fully aware that the essence of the Balfour Declaration has never been implemented vis-à-vis the rights of the Palestinians themselves.

To look at it from a different perspective, there is, and rightfully so, outrage when anyone denies the existence of the Holocaust. But when people deny the displacement and

---

[142] David Ben Gurion, quoted in a 1938 speech on pp 91-2 of Chomsky's Fateful Triangle: United States, Israel and the Palestinians.

persecution, even the existence of Palestine and the Palestinians, there is no indignation whatsoever. There is a clear double standard.

To summarize, Muslims believe that Israel should exist, but the rights of the Palestinians should not be overlooked in this conflict. A best-case scenario for all parties is two states living side by side in peace. Let's pray for that to happen sooner rather than later.

The "Violent" Verses of the *Qur'an*

One of the favorite tactics employed by the Islamophobes is to quote verses of the *Qur'an* out of context, and use that as proof that Islam is a violent, bloody religion.

In fact, there were strict rules in place for warfare, which meant that fighting was only against those that raised arms against Muslims.

The British historian Karen Armstrong describes the second Islamic capture of Jerusalem in these words:

"On 2 October 1187 Saladin and his army entered Jerusalem as conquerors and for the next 800 years Jerusalem would remain a Muslim city... Saladin kept his word, and conquered the city according to the highest Islamic ideals. He did not take revenge for the 1099 massacre, as the Qur'an *advised (16:127), and now that hostilities had ceased he ended the killing (2:193-194). Not a single Christian was killed and there was no plunder. The ransoms were deliberately very low..."*

Before I discuss those verses that have been portrayed as violent, readers must be aware of a few guidelines when reading the verses of the *Qur'an*.

Historical Context.

Let me give you an example that I give quite often. If I was to announce that the President of the United States has declared war on Japan, naturally people would be baffled. Questions would be asked. Why? Aren't they our allies? Didn't they go through a terrible natural disaster recently? But then I would clarify, that I was talking about the declaration of war after the attack on Pearl Harbor in 1941. There are many *Qur'anic* verses that were talking about a specific situation of the time, but are portrayed as universal and relevant today.

Surrounding Verses

It is important to read the whole chapter, or at least the surrounding verses, to get a better understanding of what the verses are actually saying. For example, one verse may be talking about waging war, but the very next verse will talk about trying to make a treaty and giving priority to peace. The Islamophobes will only mention the verse that mentions fighting, while conveniently omitting the surrounding verses encouraging peace.

So here are a few examples of verses which are portrayed as violent, and how the words are twisted by people to make them seem more violent. All of these verses were taken from an openly anti-Islamic website, and in some cases I have added the misleading comments of the website, and then explained what the verses actually mean, in the light of the surrounding verses and actual commentaries of the *Qur'an*. I have written in bold the verses that the authors of anti-Islamic websites intentionally leave out, unbeknownst to the innocent reader, who is taken in by the cherry-picked nature of the verses.

Chapter 2, Verses 190-195

The verse below was quoted from an anti-Islamic website. Quite conveniently, the words which *discourage* fighting were left out even though they are in the middle of the verse!

"And slay them wherever ye find them, and drive them out of the places whence they drove you out, for persecution is worse than slaughter, but if they desist, then lo! Allah is forgiving and merciful. And fight them until persecution is no more, and religion is for Allah."

The actual complete wording is as follows, with verses that have been skipped out, and verses that are before and after:

*"**Fight in the cause of Allah those who fight you but do not transgress limits; for Allah loveth not transgressors.** And slay them wherever ye catch them, and turn them out from where they have turned you out; for tumult and oppression are worse than slaughter; **but fight them not at the Sacred Mosque, unless they (first) fight you there; but if they fight you slay them.** Such is the reward of those who suppress faith. But if they cease, Allah is Oft-Forgiving Most Merciful. **And fight them on until there is no more tumult or oppression and there prevail justice and faith in Allah; but if they cease let there be no hostility except to those who practice oppression.** The prohibited month—for the prohibited month—and so for all things prohibited there is the law*

*of equality. **If then anyone transgresses the prohibition against you, transgress ye likewise against him. But fear Allah and know that Allah is with those who restrain themselves.** And spend of your substance in the cause of Allah, and make not your own hands contribute to (your) destruction; **but do good; for Allah loveth those who do good.**"*[143]

I have added emphasis to the wording that gives a completely different picture when quoted fully. If you read it, you will see that the fighting is only allowed when fought against first, it is only to prevent oppression, and transgression (in the form of oppression, raping, pillaging etc.) during the course of warfare is strictly prohibited.

The above verses were the first to be revealed authorizing the use of force against people who threatened to harm the Prophet and his companions. Bear in mind that this authorization took place thirteen years after the call to Islam started, even though the first thirteen years were full of unyielding persecution against the minority of Muslims. Even then, the order is to fight when fought against, not to be oppressive, and not be hostile to those that had no inclination towards fighting.

Chapter 2, Verse 244

"Then fight in the cause of Allah, and know that Allah Heareth and knoweth all things."

---

[143] The Holy *Qur'an*, Chapter 2, Verses 190-195

This verse is the middle of the story of the children of Israel, specifically Samuel, according to commentators of the *Qur'an*. The critics of this verse did not mention the story related to this verse, which was about Israelites. We can assume from this that fighting for a good cause, namely a just war, has been ordained by God for all previous nations, if and when it is necessary. The Israelites were also obligated to fight to defend their religion and to suppress persecution. However the anti-Islamic website doesn't mention the historical context of the verse, nor the story about which the verse is being mentioned.

Chapter 2, Verse 216

"Fighting is enjoined on you, and it is an object of dislike to you; and it may be that you dislike a thing while it is good for you, and it may be that you love a thing while it is evil for you, and Allah knows, while you do not know."

The full text of surrounding verses is as follows:

"Do you think that you will enter Paradise while you have not yet been visited by (difficult) circumstances like those that were faced by the people who passed away before you? They were afflicted by hardship and suffering, and were so shaken down that the prophet, and those who believed with him, started saying: "When (will come) the help of Allah?" (Then, they were comforted by the Prophet who said to them) 'Behold, the help of Allah is near.' *They ask you as to what they should spend. Say: "Whatever good you spend should be for parents, kinsmen, orphans, the needy and the wayfarer; and whatever good you do, Allah* is all-aware of it." *Fighting is enjoined upon you, while it is hard on you. It could be that you dislike something, when it is good for you; and it could be that you like something when it is bad for you. Allah knows, and you do not know.* **They ask you about the Sacred Month, that is, about fighting in it.** **Say, "Fighting in it is something grave, but it is much more grave, in the sight of Allah, to prevent (people) from the path of Allah, to disbelieve in Him, and in Al-Masjid-ul-Haraam, and to expel its people from there, and Fitnah (to create disorder) is more grave than killing." They will go on fighting you until they turn you away from your faith if they could,** *while whoever of you turns away from his faith and dies an infidel, such people are those whose deeds will go to waste in this world and in the Hereafter, and they are people of the Fire. They shall be there forever.*[144]

If we pay attention to the beginning of these verses, we will find that Muslims while going through huge amounts of hardship because of the oppression that was being handed down to them by the people of Mecca. So to fight this oppression, Muslims were ordained to fight. A question that came up during those times was about the permissibility of fighting in the "Sacred months". Traditionally, it was not allowed to fight in four months of the calendar. The answer to this question is mentioned here, that if the fighting *is initiated* by the opposing party, then raising arms against them would not be problematic. The reason for this is clearly mentioned in the verse, that creating disorder and chaos in society is worse

---

[144] The Holy *Qur'an*, Chapter 2, Verses 214-217

than fighting. To quell disorder, fighting had to be taken up, even though fighting was not the objective.

Again, when the context of the verse is clarified, a different picture emerges from the one portrayed by critics of Islam.

Chapter 3, Verse 56

An anti-Islamic website quotes only this portion:

"As to those who reject faith, I will punish them with terrible agony in this world and in the Hereafter, nor will they have anyone to help."

The full actual text is as follows:

"And when Allah said: O Isa (Jesus), I am going to terminate the period of your stay (on earth) and cause you to ascend unto Me and purify you of those who disbelieve and make those who follow you above those who disbelieve to the day of resurrection; then to Me shall be your return, so l will decide between you concerning that in which you differed. As to those who reject faith, I will punish them with terrible agony in this world and in the Hereafter, nor will they have anyone to help."

As you can see, the verses in question were revealed about the Prophet Jesus, where God addresses him and explains the guidelines of faith. Those guidelines of faith have been the same with every single Messenger from God, they have never changed. Conveniently the anti-Islamic critics omitted the point that the verses were addressing Jesus! If one actually looks into the Bible, such verses of punishment can be found quite easily; punishment towards criminals is not monopolized by the *Qur'an*.[145]

Chapter 3, Verse 151

"Soon shall We cast terror into the hearts of the Unbelievers, for that they joined companions with Allah, for which He had sent no authority".

The full text is as follows:

"O ye who believe! if ye obey those who disbelieve, they will make you turn back on your heels, and ye turn back as losers. But Allah is your Protector, and He is the Best of Helpers. We shall cast terror into the hearts of those who disbelieve because they ascribe unto Allah partners, for which no warrant hath been revealed. Their habitation is the Fire, and hapless the abode of the wrong-doers."[146]

Similar to the above verses in which punishment has been mentioned for those that do not accept the guidelines for faith, these verses also mention the same punishment. One of the consequences of not having faith is that one becomes a coward, and this is the reason the polytheists have been described as having terror in their hearts.

In fact, cowardice and lack of faith going hand in hand has been clearly mentioned in the Bible:

---

[145] http://en.wikipedia.org/wiki/Christian_views_on_Hell
[146] The Holy *Qur'an*, Verses 149-151

"And he said to them, "Why are you afraid, O you of little faith?" Then he rose and rebuked the winds and the sea, and there was a great calm."[147]

"The wicked flee when no one pursues, but the righteous are bold as a lion."[148]

"One man of you puts to flight a thousand, since it is the Lord your God who fights for you, just as he promised you."[149] In this verse, one faithful main is equal to a thousand without faith in bravery.

"And as for those of you who are left, I will send faintness into their hearts in the lands of their enemies. The sound of a driven leaf shall put them to flight, and they shall flee as one flees from the sword, and they shall fall when none pursues."[150]

To summarize, the terror that is mentioned in the verse is indicative of the lack of faith of the people, not because Islam terrorizes them.

Chapter 4, Verse 74

The anti-Islamic website simply quotes verse 74.

"Let those fight in the way of Allah who sell the life of this world for the other. Whoso fighteth in the way of Allah, be he slain or be he victorious, on him We shall bestow a vast reward."

---

[147] Matthew 8:26
[148] Proverbs 28:1
[149] Joshua 23:10
[150] Leviticus 26:36

The website even goes on to say: "The martyrs of Islam are unlike the early Christians, led meekly to the slaughter. These Muslims are killed in battle, as they attempt to inflict death and destruction for the cause of Allah. Here is the theological basis for today's suicide bombers."

Now let us look at the verse 74 put into context with the surrounding verses:

"So, those who sell the worldly life for the Hereafter should fight in the way of Allah. Whoever fights in the way of Allah, then gets killed or prevails, We shall give a great reward to him. **What has happened to you that you do not fight in the way of Allah, and for the oppressed among men, women and children who say, "Our Lord, take us out from this town whose people are cruel, and make for us a supporter from Your own, and make for us a helper from Your own."** *The believers fight in the way of Allah, and the disbelievers fight in the way of Taghut. So, fight the friends of Satan. No doubt, the guile of Satan is feeble.* "[151] (Emphasis added)

The very next verse, Verse 75, which has been put into bold text above, tells us the actual reason for the fighting mentioned in verse 74, which was to help the oppressed and persecuted men, women and children in places where they were being killed, raped, and mutilated, if this kind of heartless treatment is going on in any place in the world. The anti-Islamic website portrays the verses as the "theological basis for today's suicide

---

[151] The Holy *Qur'an*, Chapter 4, Verses 74-76

bombers". The *Qur'an* itself says otherwise, but of course the real facts, in the very next verse, are concealed to make Islam look like an evil and heartless religion.

Chapter 4, Verse 89

The anti-Islamic website quotes the following:

"They but wish that ye should reject Faith, as they do, and thus be on the same footing (as they): But take not friends from their ranks until they flee in the way of Allah (From what is forbidden). But if they turn renegades, seize them and slay them wherever ye find them; and (in any case) take no friends or helpers from their ranks."

The full context with surrounding verses is as follows:

"So, what is the matter with you that you have become two groups about the hypocrites, while Allah has reverted them because of what they did? Do you want to guide the one whom Allah has let go astray? The one whom Allah lets go astray, you shall never find a way for him. They wish that you should disbelieve, as they have disbelieved, and thus you become all alike. So, do not take friends from among them unless they migrate in the way of Allah. Then, if they turn away, seize them, and kill them wherever you find them, and do not take from among them a friend or helper. **Except those who join a group between whom and you there is a treaty, or who come to you with their hearts feeling discomfort in fighting either against you or against their own people. If Allah had so willed, He would have given them power over you, then they would have fought you ; so, if they stay away from you, and do not fight you and offer you peace, then Allah has not given you**

any authority against them. You will find others who want to be secure from you, and secure from their own people. (But) whenever they are called back to the mischief, they are plunged into it. So, if they do not stay away from you, and do not offer peace to you, and do not restrain their hands, then seize them, and kill them wherever you find them, and, We have given you an open authority against them."[152]

These verses are regarding the hypocrites who claimed to be Muslims, but internally they were hailing disbelief. Time after time, they put hindrances in the path of the Muslims, sometimes causing internal divisions in the ranks between the Muslims. Fighting against these people was sanctioned in these verses, but only if these hypocrites continued to cause trouble with the Muslims. They were even protected if they joined forces with any group of people that had a treaty with the Muslims. As the bold writing above indicates, "Except those who join a group between whom and you there is a treaty, or who come to you with their hearts feeling discomfort in fighting either against you or against their own people. If Allah had so willed, He would have given them power over you, then they would have fought you; so, if they stay away from you, and do not fight you and offer you peace, then Allah has not given you any authority against them."

---

[152] The Holy *Qur'an*, Chapter 4, Verses 88-91

As you can see one more time, if the verses are taken in their full context, they portray a completely different meaning to the one that is claimed by the critics of Islam.

Chapter 4, Verse 95

The anti-Islamic website quotes this verse:

"Not equal are those believers who sit (at home) and receive no hurt, and those who strive and fight in the cause of Allah with their goods and their persons. Allah hath granted a grade higher to those who strive and fight with their goods and persons than to those who sit (at home). Unto all (in Faith) Hath Allah promised good: But those who strive and fight Hath He distinguished above those who sit (at home) by a special reward."

Here is the full section with the verses before the verse in question:

"Whoever kills a believer deliberately, his reward is Jahannam (Hell) where he shall remain forever, and Allah shall be angry with him and shall cast curse upon him, and He has prepared for him a mighty punishment. O you who believe, when you go out in the way of Allah, be careful, and do not say to the one who offers you the Salam (salutation), "You are not a believer" to seek stuff of the worldly life. So, with Allah there are spoils in abundance. In the same state you were before; then Allah favored you. So, be careful. Surely, Allah is All-Aware of what you do. Those among the believers who sit back, except the handicapped, are not equal to those who fight in the way of Allah with their riches and their lives. Allah has raised the rank of those who*

*fight with their riches and their lives, over those who sit; and to each, Allah has promised good. Allah has given precedence to those who fight over those who sit in giving them a great reward. **High ranks from Him and forgiveness and mercy. Allah is Most-Forgiving, Very-Merciful.** "*[153]

In the first verse, killing has been condemned by the *Qur'an*. The reason for the revelation of this verse was that on some occasions, during warfare even though people declared that they had become Muslim, some companions of the prophet killed them. This verse condemns such people to severe punishment. We can derive from this that the purpose of Islam was not to kill people. It was to propagate the true religion, as it was propagated by all the messengers sent by God. In the same context, the fighting that has been mentioned in the verses that come later referred to fighting those people that stood in the way of the propagation of truth, as they were hindering people from obtaining eternal salvation, and hence paving the way for their inevitable destruction in the hereafter.

Chapter 4, Verse 104

This is the portion of the verses which have been quoted by the anti-Islamic website:

"And be not weak hearted in pursuit of the enemy; if you suffer pain, then surely they (too) suffer pain as you suffer pain..."

---

[153] The Holy *Qur'an*, Chapter 4, Verses 93-96

The same website goes on to say, criticizing the verse, " Is pursuing an injured and retreating enemy really an act of self-defense?"

As usual, the way that this verse has been interpreted is completely incorrect. This verse was revealed when the Muslims had taken severe losses at the battle of Uhud. Seventy of the companions of Prophet Muhammad had been killed in the battle, as a result of which the rest of the companions were feeling disillusioned and disheartened. So this verse was revealed to revive their spirits, with the wording stating that in warfare there will always be people hurt from both sides, therefore there is no need to feel disheartened. There is no mention anywhere of pursuing injured soldiers!

Chapter 5, Verse 33

Here is the verse demonstrated on the anti-Islamic website:

"The punishment of those who wage war against Allah and His messenger and strive to make mischief in the land is only this, that they should be murdered or crucified or their hands and their feet should be cut off on opposite sides or they should be imprisoned; this shall be as a disgrace for them in this world, and in the hereafter they shall have a grievous chastisement."

Here is the whole section, with verses before and after the verse in question:

"For this reason, We decreed for the children of Isra'il that whoever kills a person not in retaliation for a person killed, nor (as a punishment) for spreading disorder on the earth, is as if he has killed the whole of humankind, and whoever saves the life of a person is as if he has saved the life of the whole of humankind. Certainly, Our messengers have come to them with clear signs. Then, after all that, many of them are there to commit excesses on the earth. Those who fight against Allah and His Messenger and run about trying to spread disorder on the earth, their punishment is no other than that they shall be killed, or be crucified, or their hands and legs be cut off from different sides, or they be kept away from the land (they live in). That is a humiliation for them in this world, and for them there is a great punishment in the Hereafter; **except those who repent before you overpower them. Then, be sure that Allah is Most-Forgiving, Very-Merciful.**"[154] (Emphasis added).*

This verse is often portrayed as describing anyone who opposes Islam. The reality is described by commentators of the *Qur'an*, that say that it refers to bandits and thugs that rob people. They "wage war against Allah and his Messenger" because they go against the command of God and all his Messengers prohibiting them from stealing.

Once again, we can see that conveniently omitting the verses before and after don't give the full picture. And when we refer to commentaries of the Quran, another picture emerges. The

---

[154] The Holy *Qur'an*, Verses 32-34

verse before (in bold) condemns killing, equating one life to the life of all humanity. The verse after (also in bold) says that if the criminal repents, there is to be no punishment.

Chapter 8, Verse 12

Here is the edited verse on the anti-Islamic website:

"I will cast terror into the hearts of those who disbelieve. Therefore strike off their heads and strike off every fingertip of them."

Here is the full verse:

"When your Lord revealed to the angels: "I am with you. So, make firm the feet of those who believe. I shall cast awe into the hearts of those who disbelieve. So, strike at the necks, and strike at every finger-joint of theirs.""

It is *not* a blanket statement for Muslims to strike at the necks and fingertips of the disbelievers. It is God, talking to the angels, *not* the Muslims, at the Battle of *Badr*, to assist the weaker forces of the Muslim army against the Quraish. So therefore it is taken out of context to make it look like it is a universal statement of Islam, giving the perception that Muslims should be killing all disbelievers at all times. It was simply a specific verse, talking about a specific point in history, and it was only for that time.

Remember also that the Battle of Badr was the first battle that was authorized by the *Qur'an* in Islamic history, despite thirteen years of persecution in Mecca. The Muslims were outnumbered three-to-one, with very minimal resources, yet they won resoundingly.

Chapter 8, Verse 15

The anti-Islamic website quotes the verse:

"O ye who believe! When ye meet those who disbelieve in battle, turn not your backs to them. Whoso on that day turneth his back to them, unless maneuvering for battle or intent to join a company, he truly hath incurred wrath from Allah, and his habitation will be hell, a hapless journey's end."

This verse is in line with literally all military policies in the world for soldiers stationed in a war zone who desert their post. According to the Universal Code of Military Justice, Article 85, desertion during the time of war can be punishable by death.

Here are the punishments listed under Article 85 for the crime of desertion:

(1) *Completed or attempted desertion with intent to avoid hazardous duty or to shirk important service.* Dishonorable discharge, forfeiture of all pay and allowances, and confinement for 5 years.

(2) *Other cases of completed or attempted desertion.*

(a) *Terminated by apprehension.* Dishonorable discharge, forfeiture of all pay and allowances, and confinement for 3 years.

(b) *Terminated otherwise.* Dishonorable discharge, forfeiture of all pay and allowances, and confinement for 2 years.

(3) *In time of war.* **Death or such other punishment as a court-martial may direct.**[155] (Emphasis added).

When this is the ruling for the modern United States military, then quoting verses from the *Qur'an* making it seem like it's uniquely an Islamic thing to be strict with military deserters is disingenuous to say the least.

Chapter 8, Verse 39

Here is the verse on an anti-Islamic website:

"And fight with them until there is no more *fitna* (disorder, unbelief) and religion should be only for Allah"

And here is the verse with surrounding verses, giving a completely different picture:

Say to those who disbelieve that if they desist (from infidelity), they shall be forgiven for what has passed (of their sins), and if they repeat, then, the precedent of the earlier people is already

---

[155] http://www.ucmj.us/sub-chapter-10-punitive-articles/885-article-85-desertion

established (that the infidels are punished). And fight them until there is no *Fitnah* (mischief), and total obedience becomes for Allah. **So, if they desist, then, Allah is indeed watchful over what they do. And if they turn away, then, rest assured that Allah is your protector. So excellent a protector is He, and so excellent a supporter.**[156](Emphasis added)

It's amazing that a completely different picture emerges when the surrounding verses are included. In fact, the anti-Islamic websites are so dishonest, they didn't even write the complete verse, because the complete verse clearly shows that if the people are not fighting you, you are not supposed to fight them!

The prior verses (in bold) talk about forgiveness of sins, and the end of the same verse and the next verse talks about laying down arms against those that don't fight. Again this proves without a shadow of doubt that Islam discourages fighting unless fought against.

Chapter 8, Verse 57

Here is the verse as presented on the anti-Islamic website:

"If thou comest on them in the war, deal with them so as to strike fear in those who are behind them, that haply they may remember."

Here is the same verse with surrounding verses:

---

[156] The Holy *Qur'an*, Chapter 8, Verses 38-40

"Those with whom you have entered into a treaty, then they break their treaty each time, and they do not fear Allah. So, if you find them in war, deal with them in a way that those behind them have to disperse fearfully, so that they take a lesson. *And if you apprehend a breach from a people, then, throw (the treaty) towards them in straight-forward terms. Surely, Allah does not like those who breach the trust. The disbelievers should never think that they have surpassed (the divine punishment). Surely, they cannot frustrate (the Divine will). Prepare against them whatever force you can, and the trained horses whereby you frighten Allah's enemy and your own enemy and others besides them whom you do not know. Allah knows them. Whatever thing you spend in the way of Allah, it will be paid to you in full, and you shall not be wronged. And if they tilt towards peace, you too should tilt towards it, and place your trust in Allah. Surely, He is the All-Hearing, the All-Knowing. If they intend to deceive you, then, Allah is all-sufficient for you."*[157]

The verse, number 57 has been portrayed by the anti-Islamic website to show that Muslims are supposed to be severe with everyone, and strike fear into people's hearts. But the surrounding verses show clearly that it is referring to those people that break treaties with the Muslims, and subsequently fight against them. It is *not* referring to the general peace-loving public. Amazingly, verse 61 (in bold) goes on to say that if those same people who are fighting against you lean towards

---

[157] The Holy *Qur'an*, Chapter 8, verses 56-61

peace, you should accept their inclination and also accept peace, while placing your trust in God.

Chapter 8, Verses 59-60

This verse was mentioned above. This is how the anti-Islamic website portrays it:

"And let not those who disbelieve suppose that they can outstrip (Allah's Purpose). Lo! they cannot escape. Make ready for them all thou canst of (armed) force and of horses tethered, that thereby ye may dismay the enemy of Allah and your enemy."

As I have mentioned in the previous section, verse 61 exhorts people to accept peace treaties:

"And if they tilt towards peace, you too should tilt towards it, and place your trust in Allah. Surely, He is the All-Hearing, the All-Knowing."

But very conveniently, the anti-Islamic website cherry-picked the verses that don't talk about peace, and miss the verses denoting peace even though it's the very next verse! It is a blatant example of academic fraud at its worst!

Chapter 8, Verse 65

The anti-Islamic website very disingenuously only mentions a small portion of a lengthy verse:

"O Prophet, exhort the believers to fight..."

The actual verse is as follows:

"O Prophet, rouse the believers to fighting. If there are twenty among you, who are patient, they will overcome two hundred; and if there are one hundred among you, they will overcome one thousand of those who disbelieve, because they are a people who do not understand. Now Allah has lightened your burden, and He knew that there is weakness in you. So, if there are one hundred among you, who are patient, they will overcome two hundred; and if there are one thousand among you, they will overcome two thousand by the will of Allah. Allah is with the patient."[158]

If you look at the verse in its complete sense, you will discover that the Prophet is being encouraged, as a suppressed minority, to fight against the oppressive army that is greater in number many-fold. But of course the anti-Islamic critics wouldn't want the public to know that the fighting is being encouraged against an oppressive regime, a brutal army etc., and *not* the general public. So the beginning of the verse is quoted, leaving the important remainder of the verse out.

Chapter 9, Verse 5

Here is the quoted verse on the anti-Islamic website:

"So when the sacred months have passed away, then slay the idolaters wherever you find them, and take them captives and besiege them and lie in wait for them in every ambush, then if

---

[158] The Holy *Qur'an*, Chapter 8, Verse 65-66

they repent and keep up prayer and pay the poor-rate, leave their way free to them."

Here is the actual verse, with surrounding verses:

"Except those of the polytheists with whom you have a treaty, and they were not deficient (in fulfilling the treaty) with you, and did not back up any one against you. So fulfill the treaty with them up to their term. Surely, Allah loves the God-fearing. So, when the sacred months expire, kill the Mushriks wherever you find them, and catch them and besiege them and sit in ambush for them everywhere. Then, if they repent and establish Salah and pay Zakah, leave their way. **Surely, Allah is most Forgiving, Very-Merciful. And if any one of the polytheists seeks your protection, give him protection until he listens to the Word of Allah, then let him reach his place of safety; That is because they are a people who do not know."**

Verse 3 (in bold) says that anyone who has a treaty with the Muslims, that treaty must be honored, as long as the treaty is not broken by the opposing party. Verse 6 (also in bold) says that if any of the polytheists seeks protection, then give him that protection, and even take these people to a place of safety, where they will be free from harm. Obviously quoting only Verse 5 gives a derogatory picture of Islam, which is what the Islamophobes undoubtedly want to achieve; to give Islam a negative portrayal so that it is looked down upon by all humanity.

Chapter 9, Verse 14

The anti-Islamic website quotes this portion of a verse:

"Fight them, Allah will punish them by your hands and bring them to disgrace..."

The actual verses are:

"Would you not fight a people who broke their oaths and conspired to expel the Messenger, and it was they who started (fighting) against you for the first time? Do you fear them? But Allah has greater right that you fear Him, if you are believers. Fight them, so that Allah should punish them at your hands and disgrace them, **and help you win against them and bring relief to bosoms of the believing people"**[159]

The verse before (in bold) clearly states that the fighting is against those people that broke their treaties, conspired to expel the Prophet, and they initiated the fighting! Once again, a clearer picture emerges about the true intent of the verses when the whole verses are displayed. Of course the anti-Islamic crowd doesn't want us to know that, preferring to keep us in the dark about what the *Qur'an* actually says.

Chapter 9, Verse 20

The anti-Islamic website quotes this verse:

"Those who believe, and have left their homes and striven with their wealth and their lives in Allah's way are of much greater worth in

---

[159] The Holy *Qur'an*, Verses 13-14

Allah's sight. These are they who are triumphant." The website follows the quote with: *"The "striving" spoken of here is Jihad".*

The actual verses are as follows:

"In fact, the mosques of Allah are built-up only by those who believe in Allah and the Last Day and those who establish Salah and pay Zakah and who fear none but Allah. So, it is hoped that they are to be among those on the right path. Have you taken the serving of water to the pilgrims and the maintenance of Al-Masjid-ul-Haraam as equal to (the acts) of one who believes in Allah and in the Last Day, and carries out Jihad in the way of Allah? They are not equal in the sight of Allah. Allah does not lead the wrongdoing people to the right path. Those who believed and emigrated and carried out Jihad in the way of Allah with their wealth and lives are greater in rank in the sight of Allah, and it is they who are the successful. Their Lord gives them the happy news of Mercy from Him, and of (His) Pleasure, and of Gardens having an everlasting bliss for them, where they shall dwell forever. Surely, it is Allah with whom lies a great reward."[160]

If we look at the verses before this particular verse, they are talking about spending wealth in building mosques, serving of water to pilgrims etc. In the same context, reference to *jihad* is in spending wealth and energy for the promotion of the religion of Islam. We have already mentioned that the linguistic meaning of *jihad* is "to strive". Here the "striving" is exemplified by spending one's wealth.

---

[160] The Holy *Qur'an*, Chapter 9, verses 18-22

Chapter 9, Verse 29

The anti-Islamic website says the following:

"Fight those who believe not in Allah nor the Last Day, nor hold that forbidden which hath been forbidden by Allah and His Messenger, nor acknowledge the religion of Truth, (even if they are) of the People of the Book, until they pay the Jizya with willing submission, and feel themselves subdued."

The anti-Islamic website goes on to say, *""People of the Book" refers to Christians and Jews. This was one of the final "revelations" from Allah and it set in motion the tenacious military expansion, in which Muhammad's companions managed to conquer two-thirds of the Christian world in just the next 100 years. Islam is intended to dominate all other people and faiths."*

To understand the true meaning of this verse, we must know the context in which it was revealed. It was revealed prior to the expedition of *Tabuk*, which was to fight against the superpower of the time, the Roman Empire. The purpose of the strong words was to make sure the Muslim army would not be overawed by the strength of the mighty Romans. Virtually all commentators of the *Qur'an* agree that this was when the verse was revealed.

I will talk about the Jizya later on, in the chapter entitled *Dhimmi...What does it Mean?*

Chapter 9, Verse 30

The anti-Islamic website quotes the following verse:

"And the Jews say: Ezra is the son of Allah; and the Christians say: The Messiah is the son of Allah; these are the words of their mouths; they imitate the saying of those who disbelieved before; may Allah destroy them; how they are turned away!"

The same verse, with the following verses included, reads:

"The Jews say, "'Uzair (Ezra) is the Son of Allah" and the Christians say, "Jesus (the Christ) is the Son of Allah." That is their oral statement. They imitate the saying of the earlier disbelievers. May Allah ruin them, how far they are turned back from the truth! **They have taken their rabbis and their monks as gods beside Allah, and also (they have taken) Jesus the son of Maryam (as god). And they were not commanded but to worship only One God. There is no god but He. Pure is He from what they associate with Him. They wish to blow out the Light of Allah with their mouths, and Allah rejects everything short of making His light perfect, no matter how the disbelievers may hate it. He is the One who has sent down His Messenger with guidance and the Faith of Truth, so that He makes it prevail over every faith, no matter how the Mushriks may hate it. O you who believe, many of the rabbis and the monks do eat up the wealth of the people by false means and prevent (them) from the way of Allah. As for those who accumulate**

gold and silver and do not spend it in the way of Allah, give them the 'good' news of a painful punishment."[161]

At this juncture, I will request my Jewish and Christian friends and readers not to be offended with what I am about to say, as the purpose is not to hurt anyone, it's to get what Muslims believe to be the facts out to the general public, in the light of the above statement of the *Qur'an*.

Firstly, many Jews will take issue with the statement that Jews believed Ezra to be son of God. This statement was talking about specific tribes of Jews that lived in Arabia at the time of the Prophet, and was not a belief adopted by the majority of the Jewish people. So this verse was referring to that specific tribe, not Jews in general.

The Christians and Jews will both take issue with the statement that says that they took their rabbis and monks as Gods besides Allah, so it needs some clarification. What this verse means is that when the rabbis and monks gave rulings contrary to the clear teachings of the scripture, those contradictory rulings were given precedence over the scripture; therefore, they regarded the rulings of the rabbis and monks as more important than the rulings of God, and adopted them as religious rulings without any dispute. So in essence, their adopting of the rules of their religious leaders over the rules of

---

[161] The Holy *Qur'an*, Chapter 9, Verses 30-34

God made the religious leaders Gods in their eyes. This is what the verse means.

If you look at the Christian and Jewish faiths today, you will find that this rings true, that the secondary teachings are adopted over the teachings of God. Amongst the Jews, the teachings of Rabbinic Law from the Talmud are given more priority than the Torah itself.

Amongst Christians, the belief and teachings of Paul are adopted over the teachings of Jesus; this is a disputed issue even within today's Christian denominations.

Chapter 9, Verses 38-39.

The anti-Islamic website has the following quote:

"O ye who believe! What is the matter with you, that, when ye are asked to go forth in the cause of Allah, ye cling heavily to the earth? Do ye prefer the life of this world to the Hereafter? But little is the comfort of this life, as compared with the Hereafter. Unless ye go forth, He will punish you with a grievous penalty, and put others in your place."

The actual verses, including those before, are as follows:

"Surely, the number of months according to Allah is twelve (as written) in the Book of Allah on the day He created the heavens and the Earth, of which there are Four Sacred Months. That is the right faith. So, do not wrong yourself therein. And fight the Mushriks all together, as they fight you all together, and be sure that Allah is with the God-fearing. Nasi' (i.e. postponement of months) is nothing but a

further excess in infidelity, whereby the disbelievers are misguided. They allow it one year and disallow it another year, so that they may conform (only) to the number of what Allah has sanctified, and allow what Allah has disallowed. The evil of their deeds has been beautified for them (by Satan). And Allah does not lead the disbelieving people to the right path. O you who believe, what is wrong with you that when it is said to you, "Come out in the way of Allah," you turn heavy (and cling) to the ground. Have you become happy with the worldly life instead of the Hereafter? So, (remember that) the enjoyment of the worldly life is but trivial in (comparison with) the Hereafter. If you do not march forth (in the way of Allah), He will chastise you with a painful punishment and will replace you with another nation, and you can do Him no harm at all. Allah is powerful to do anything."[162]

Once again, we need to go back just a couple of verses, and we find that fighting is ordained for those people are fighting against the Muslims, as can be seen in the verse that has been written in bold.

Chapter 9, Verse 41

"Go forth, light-armed and heavy-armed, and strive with your wealth and your lives in the way of Allah! That is best for you if ye but knew." See also the verse that follows (9:42) - "If there had been immediate gain (in sight), and the journey easy, they would (all) without doubt have followed thee, but the distance was long, (and weighed) on them."

---

[162] The Holy *Qur'an*, Chapter 9, Verses 36-39

These verses follow the above mentioned verses 38 and 39, so there is no need to explain them further. They are talking about the same subject.

Chapter 9, Verse 73

The anti-Islamic website quotes the following:

"O Prophet! Strive hard against the unbelievers and the hypocrites and be unyielding to them; and their abode is hell, and evil is the destination."

The actual wording is:

"O Prophet, carry out Jihad (struggle) against the disbelievers and hypocrites, and be strict with them. And their abode is Jahannam (Hell), and it is an evil terminus. **They swear by Allah that they said nothing, while indeed, they had said the word of infidelity and had disbelieved after having accepted Islam, and had intended what they could not achieve. And they have reacted for nothing but that Allah and His Messenger have enriched them with His grace. So, if they repent, it will be good for them, and if they turn away, Allah will chastise them with a painful punishment in this world and the Hereafter, and for them there is neither a friend on the Earth, nor a helper."*

To get an accurate understanding of this verse, it is essential to know the background and the commentary. The words "and had intended what they could not achieve" that are in bold refer to the hypocrites that intended to kill the prophet

Muhammad.[163] The verse after that says that there was no reason for them to want that, as the only "crime" that the Prophet Muhammad had committed was to bestow them with grace and guidance to the truth.

Once again we see that fighting is only authorized against those people that want to harm and kill the Prophet Muhammad and the Muslims.

Chapter 9, Verse 88

The anti-Islamic website has the following verse:

"But the Messenger, and those who believe with him, **strive and fight** with their wealth and their persons: for them are (all) good things: and it is they who will prosper."

The actual verse does not have two words "strive and fight". This is an addition to the verse that is simply not there. The actual wording is only with the word "strive". The addition of the word "fight" gives an incorrect meaning.

The meaning of the verse, therefore, is that Muslims are required to utilize their resources, whether material or physical, to promote truth and justice.

Chapter 9, verse 111

The anti-Islamic website has the following quote:

---

[163] See Tafseer ibn Katheer for the detailed interpretation of this verse

"Allah hath purchased of the believers their persons and their goods; for theirs (in return) is the garden (of Paradise): they fight in His cause, and slay and are slain: a promise binding on Him in truth, through **the Law, the Gospel, and the Qur'an**: and who is more faithful to his covenant than Allah? Then rejoice in the bargain which ye have concluded: that is the achievement supreme."

The author of the anti-Islamic website does not specify the meaning of "the law, the Gospel, and the *Qur'an*". The actual wording used in the *Qur'an* is "the Torah, the Bible, and the Qur'an".

I have touched upon this subject before, that fighting to protect the religion and the truth was ordained by God in all the previous scriptures, including the Torah and the Bible, so the mention of it in the *Qur'an* should not seem alien to anyone.

Chapter 9, verse 123

The anti-Islamic website has the following:

"O you who believe! Fight those of the unbelievers who are near to you and let them find in you hardness."

The actual wording is:

"O you who believe, fight those disbelievers **who are near you**, and let them find severity in you. Know well that Allah is with the God-fearing. When a Surah is sent down, some of them (the hypocrites) say, "Whose faith from among you has been increased by this?" So far as the believers are concerned, it has certainly increased their faith, and *they are quite happy. As for those who have malady in their hearts, it adds further impurity to their (initial) impurity, and they die infidels. Do they not see that they are put to trial every year once or twice; still they neither repent, nor do they take lesson? And when a Surah is sent down, they look at each other (as if saying): "Is there someone watching you?" Then they turn away. Allah has turned their hearts, because they are a people who do not understand. **Surely, there has come to you, from your midst, a Messenger who feels it very hard on him if you face a hardship and who is very anxious for your welfare, and for the believers he is very kind, very merciful. So, if they turn away, say (O Messenger,) "Enough for me is Allah. There is no god but He. In Him I have placed my trust, and He is the Lord of the Great Throne."*"[164]

This verse is referring to the hypocrites that were in the midst of the Muslims, and will always on the lookout for opportunities to harm the prophet Muhammad and his followers. It is those hypocrites that are mentioned in this verse, and the wording "who are near you" indicates that it is not a general ruling; it is limited to those hypocrites who were in the midst of the Muslims.

If you look at the last two verses in this section, you will find that the prophet Muhammad is described as, " *a Messenger who feels it very hard on him if you face a hardship, who is very anxious for your welfare, and for the believers he is very kind, very merciful.*" It wouldn't make sense to order people to fight on the one hand,

---

[164] The Holy *Qur'an*, Chapter 9, Verses 123-129.

and then describe the mercy and compassion of the prophet Muhammad. This also proves that the reference was towards specific hypocrites who gave Muslims a hard time, and would have even killed the Muslims if they had been given the opportunity.

Furthermore, the final verse indicates that if the people do not want to accept Islam, then they should be left to God to be judged.

Chapter 17, verse 16

The anti-Islamic website quotes the following:

"And when We wish to destroy a town, We send Our commandment to the people of it who lead easy lives, but they transgress therein; thus the word proves true against it, so We destroy it with utter destruction."

The same website claims the following:

"Note that the crime is moral transgression, and the punishment is "utter destruction." (Before ordering the 9/11 attacks, Osama bin Laden first issued Americans an invitation to Islam)."

The actual wording of the *Qur'an* is as follows:

*"Whoever adopts the right path does so for his own benefit, and whoever goes astray does so to his own detriment, and no bearer of burden shall bear the burden of another, **and it is not Our way to punish (anyone) unless We send a Messenger.** And when We intend to*

destroy a habitation, We command its affluent people (to do good), then they commit sins therein, and thus the word (of punishment) becomes applicable to it (habitation), and We annihilate it totally. **How many a generation have We destroyed after Noah! And enough is your Lord to know, (and) watch the sins of His servants.**"[165]

The anti-Islamic website implies that the verse is an open invitation for terrorists to destroy mankind. But the actual background to the verses is the historical outcome of nations that refused to listen to the call of their messengers. This is clarified by the next verse, which talks about the flood of Noah, which is in accordance with the story of the Great Flood that is told in the Old Testament.

So to summarize, the verses in question are *not* authorizing Muslims to destroy villages and townships, it refers to the punishment of God descending on those places that do not adhere to the teachings of their messengers. This is completely in line with the teachings of the Bible, which talks about the punishment given by God to various nations because of their disobedience.

Chapter 18, Verses 65-81

The anti-Islamic website claims the following:

---

[165] The Holy *Qur'an*, Chapter 17, Verses 15-17

"This parable lays the theological groundwork for honor killings, in which a family member is murdered because they brought shame to the family, either through apostasy or perceived moral indiscretion. The story (which is not found in any Jewish or Christian source) tells of Moses encountering a man with "special knowledge" who does things which don't seem to make sense on the surface, but are then justified according to later explanation. One such action is to murder a youth for no apparent reason (74). However, the wise man later explains that it was feared that the boy would "grieve" his parents by "disobedience and ingratitude." He was killed so that Allah could provide them a 'better' son. (Note: This is one reason why honor killing is sanctioned by Shariah. Reliance of the Traveler (Umdat al-Saliq) says that punishment for murder is not applicable when a parent or grandparent kills their offspring.)"

I will deal with the issue of honor killings in a special chapter. For now, let us say that the claims made by the website are completely false. The parable referred to here is the story of Moses and Khidr, which has never been adopted by a single Islamic Jurist to derive any rulings of Islamic jurisprudence.

Chapter 25, Verse 52

The anti-Islamic website quotes:

"Therefore listen not to the Unbelievers, but strive against them with the utmost strenuousness..."

The same website goes on to say:

"Strive against" is Jihad - obviously not in the personal context. It's also significant to point out that this is a Meccan verse.

The actual verses are as follows:

"Had We so willed, We would have sent a (separate) warner for every town, (but, according to Our wisdom, We have sent Muhammad as a prophet for all these towns). So, (O Prophet,) do not obey the disbelievers, and strive against them with it (the Qur'an), in utmost jihad/endeavor." [166]

Commentators of the *Qur'an* have unanimously agreed that in the words "strive against them with it", the pronoun "it" refers to the *Qur'an*.[167]

We can derive two points from this:

- This verse refers to striving with the *Qur'an* as a major jihad. We can use from this that the main usage of the word jihad is for propagation and striving. Otherwise the verse will not make sense. How will you fight a war with the *Qur'an*?
- This verse was revealed in Mecca, many years before the rulings of actual physical fighting were revealed in Madinah. So the meaning could not have meant

---

[166] The Holy *Qur'an*, Chapter 25, Verses 51-52
[167] Ibn Kathir, Zamakhshari, Tabari etc were the commentaries reviewed

physical warfare. Again we see that the use of the word jihad is utilized to denote peaceful propagation.

Chapter 33, verses 60-62

"If the hypocrites, and those in whose hearts is a disease, and the alarmists in the city do not cease, We verily shall urge thee on against them, then they will be your neighbors in it but a little while. Accursed, they will be seized wherever found and slain with a (fierce) slaughter." Although the website lists verse 62, it is not written.

The wording, including the next verse, is as follows:

"If the hypocrites and those having malady in their hearts and the ones who spread rumors in Madinah do not stop (their evil deeds), We will certainly stir you up against them, then they shall no longer live in it as your neighbors, but for a little while. And that too in a state of being) accursed. Wherever they are found, they shall be seized, and shall be killed thoroughly **A consistent practice of Allah in the matter of those who have gone before. And you will never find a change in Allah's consistent practice.***"*[168]

This is one of those verses that require the reader to go through the majority of the chapter in which it occurs. In the chapter is entitled "The Confederates", and it refers to that time when all the disbelieving Arabs in the area decided in a unified way to make a united army against the Muslims. Subsequently, they surrounded the city of Madinah in a lengthy

---

[168] The Holy Quran, Chapter 33, Verses 60-62

siege. During this troubled time, the hypocrites and weak-minded people started making blunt fabricated accusations against the Prophet, claiming that he had lied to them all this time. These verses are critical of those people that were creating discord in the ranks of the Muslims.

In addition, the next verse, verse 62 clarifies that this ruling of being strict against people that create disunity has always been there, including in previous nations. Perhaps the author of the anti-Islamic website wanted to conceal this verse for the very reason, that it is not a uniquely Islamic issue?

Chapter 47, Verses 3-4

The anti-Islamic website quotes the following verse and adds the following notes:

"Those who reject Allah follow vanities, while those who believe follow the truth from their lord. Thus does Allah set forth form men their lessons by similitude. Therefore when you meet in battle those who disbelieve, then smite the necks until when you have overcome them, then make (them) prisoners," Those who reject Allah are to be subdued in battle. The verse goes on to say the only reason Allah doesn't do the dirty work himself is in order to test the faithfulness of Muslims. Those who kill pass the test. "But if it had been Allah's Will, He could certainly have exacted retribution from them (Himself); but (He lets you fight) in order to test you, some with others. But those who are slain in the Way of Allah,- He will never let their deeds be lost."

The dishonesty and lack of integrity becomes starkly apparent in this single verse.

Here is the full section, this time mentioning (in bold) what the anti-Islamic website left out:

"This because those who reject Allah follow falsehood, while those who believe follow the Truth from their Lord: Thus does Allah set forth for men their lessons by similitudes. (3) Therefore, when ye meet the Unbelievers (in fight), smite at their necks; at length, when ye have thoroughly subdued them, bind a bond firmly (on them): therefore (is the time for) either generosity or ransom: **until the war lays down its burdens. Thus (are ye commanded):** *but if it had been Allah's Will, he could certainly have exacted retribution from them (Himself); but (He lets you fight) in order to test you, some with others. But those who are slain in the way of Allah he will never let their deeds be lost."*[169]

The actual verse clearly states that fighting only continues until the opposing army lays down its weapons. Not simply stopping at that, the *Qur'an* emphasizes that this ruling is a command from God. But conveniently the anti-Islamic website left only that portion of the verse out that doesn't fulfill the anti-Islamic agenda, which is simply to portray Islam as a barbaric religion.

Chapter 47, verse 35

The anti-Islamic website quotes the following verse:

---

[169] The Holy *Qur'an*, Chapter 47, Verses 3-4

"Be not weary and faint-hearted, crying for peace, when ye should be uppermost (Shakir: "have the upper hand") for Allah is with you,"

To understand this verse in the correct context we must look at the history of when it was revealed. Imam Mawdudi, in his explanation of the Qur'an explains:

"Here, one should bear in mind the fact that when this discourse was revealed only a handful of the Muslims consisting of a couple of hundreds of the Muhajirin and Ansar living in the small town of Madinah were upholding the standard of Islam and they were not only faced by the powerful Quraish but also by the whole of pagan Arabia. Such were the conditions when they were exhorted 'not to be faint-hearted and not to beg (the enemy) for peace", but to make preparations for the decisive conflict. This does not mean that the Muslims should never negotiate for peace, but it means that in a state like this it is not right to initiate peace negotiations when it shows the Muslims' weakness, for it will still further embolden the enemy. The Muslims should first establish their superiority in power and strength; then if they negotiate peace there will be no harm."[170]

Again, when the context is understood, a clearer picture emerges about the true meaning of the verses.

---

[170] Tafheem-ul-Qur'an, English translation

Chapter 48, Verse 29

The anti-Islamic website states:

""Muhammad is the messenger of Allah. And those with him are hard (ruthless) against the disbelievers and merciful among themselves." Islam is not about treating everyone equally. There are two very distinct standards that are applied based on religious status."

Again, very conveniently, the anti-Islamic website leaves out the following portion of the verse. The actual verse is as follows:

"Muhammad is the messenger of Allah, and those who are with him are hard on the disbelievers, compassionate among themselves; you will see them bowing down in Ruku', prostrating themselves in Sajdah, seeking grace from Allah, and (His) good pleasure; their distinguishing feature is on their faces from the effect of Sajdah (prostration). This is their description in Torah; and their description in Injil (the Bible) is: like a sown crop that brings forth its shoot, then makes it strong, then it grows thick and stands straight on its stem, looking good to the farmers, so that He may enrage the disbelievers through them. Allah has promised forgiveness and a huge reward to those of them who believe and do good deeds."[171]

Amazingly, the verse is the *Qur'an* references the Torah and the Bible, which the anti-Islamic website leaves out! Scholars have

---

[171] The Holy *Qur'an*, Chapter 48, Verse 29

mentioned that the references to the Torah are found in Deuteronomy 33, Verses 1-3, and the Bible in Mark 4, Verses 26 to 29, as follows:

¹And this is the blessing, wherewith Moses the man of God blessed the children of Israel before his death.

²And he said, The LORD came from Sinai, and rose up from Seir unto them; he shined forth from mount Paran, and he came with ten thousands of saints: from his right hand went a fiery law for them.

³Yea, he loved the people; all his saints are in thy hand: and they sat down at thy feet; every one shall receive of thy words.[172]

Islamic scholars say that the words, "The Lord came from Sinai" refers to Moses, "And rose up from Seir" refers to Jesus, and "He shined forth from Mount Paran, and he came with ten thousands of saints:" until the end of verse 3 refers to the Prophet Muhammad.

The reference in the Bible is referring to Mark 4, verses 26-29. The same parable is found in Luke 13, verses 18-19, and Matthew 13, Verse 31.

"He also said, "This is what the kingdom of God is like. A man scatters seed on the ground. ²⁷Night and day, whether he sleeps or gets up, the seed sprouts and grows, though he does not know how. ²⁸ All by itself

---

[172] King James Version Bible, Deuteronomy 33, Verses 1-3

the soil produces grain—first the stalk, then the head, then the full kernel in the head. ²⁹ As soon as the grain is ripe, he puts the sickle to it, because the harvest has come."[173]

This parable is the same as found at the end of Chapter 48, verse 29 in the *Qur'an*, as mentioned above.

Amazingly, people fail to question such people who cherry-pick verses of the *Qur'an*, quote them out of context, quote part of them, all with the intention of maligning Islam.

Chapter 61, Verse 4

This is how the anti-Islamic website portrays this verse:

"Surely Allah loves those who fight in His way." Religion of Peace, indeed! This is followed by (61:9): "He it is who has sent His Messenger (Mohammed) with guidance and the religion of truth (Islam) to make it victorious over all religions even though the infidels may resist."

The website quotes Chapter 61, Verse 4, then skips a whole four verses, quoting only verse 9! Why does the author leave out all these verses? Because they make a reference to Jesus and Moses, foretelling the coming of Prophet Muhammad!

Here is the section in its entirety:

" Surely Allah loves those who fight in His way in firm rows, as if they were solid edifice. And (remember) when Musa said to his people, "O

---

[173] New International Version Bible, Mark 4, 26-29

my people, why do you hurt me, while you know that I am a messenger of Allah sent towards you." So, when they adopted deviation, Allah let their hearts become deviate. And Allah does not guide the sinful people. Remember) when 'Isa, son of Maryam, said, "O children of Isra'il, I am a messenger of Allah sent towards you, confirming the Torah that is (sent down) before me, and giving you the good news of a messenger who will come after me, whose name will be Ahmad." But when he came to them with manifest signs, they said, "This is a clear magic." And who is more unjust than the one who forges a lie against Allah, while he is invited to Islam? And Allah does not guide the unjust people. They wish to extinguish the light of Allah with their mouths, but Allah is to perfect His light, even though the disbelievers dislike (it). He is the One who has sent His Messenger with guidance and the religion of truth, so that He makes it prevail over all religions, even though the mushriks (those who ascribe partners to Allah) dislike (it).[174]

Surely by now, the readers of this book have made up their mind that all quotes that Islamophobes have mentioned negatively about the Qur'an have a clear explanation? All they have to do is actually read the Qur'an!

Chapter 61, Verse 10-12

The anti-Islamic website quotes the following verses, making a comment at the end:

---

[174] The Holy *Qur'an*, Chapter 68, Verses 4-9

"O ye who believe! Shall I lead you to a bargain that will save you from a grievous Penalty?- That ye believe in Allah and His Messenger, and that ye strive (your utmost) in the Cause of Allah, with your property and your persons: That will be best for you, if ye but knew! He will forgive you your sins, and admit you to Gardens beneath which Rivers flow, and to beautiful mansions in Gardens of Eternity." This verse was given in battle. It uses the Arabic word, Jihad."

Again, if you read the whole section, you will find reference to Jesus calling his disciples to the same "Jihad" that is mentioned in the chapter. Here is the section in its entirety.

"O you who believe, shall I tell you about a trade that saves you from a painful punishment; That you believe in Allah and His Messenger, and carry out Jihad in His way with your riches and your lives. That is much better for you, if you but know. If you do this,) He will forgive your sins, and will admit you to gardens beneath which rivers flow, and to pleasant dwellings in gardens of eternity. That is the great achievement. And (He will give you) another thing, which you love: Help from Allah, and victory, near at hand. O you who believe, be supporters of (the religion of) Allah, just as 'Isa, son of Maryam, said to the Disciples, "Who are my supporters towards Allah?" The Disciples said, "We are the supporters of (the religion of) Allah." So a group from the children of Isra'il believed, and another group disbelieved. Then We supported those who believed against their enemy, and they became victors."[175]

---

[175] The Holy *Qur'an*, Chapter 62, Verses 10-14

The conclusion is that all Prophets and Messengers, and subsequently their followers, fought to promote the truth and eradicate evil, particularly when people stood up against them to try to suppress the truth.

Cultural Issues Wrongly Associated with Islam

This chapter is dedicated to cultural issues that are portrayed as Islamic, even though they have no religious significance at all.

Because Islam is not a monolithic one-size-fits-all religion, the practitioners of the faith come from all kinds of backgrounds and nationalities Each of these factors influence a person's way of life, and contribute to the cultural aspect of that person's upbringing. Sometimes, the culture may even be at odds with Islamic teachings.

The following are just some of those examples that are at odds with the religious teachings of Islam, but are perceived to be "Islamic", just because some Muslims practice them.

"Islam Approves of Honor Killings"

The premise behind an honor killing is that because a girl in the family had an extra-marital or pre-marital affair, according to people who practice honor killings, she has "dishonored" the family, and hence must be killed.

Honor killings are *not* part of Islam. It's just sad that when a so-called Muslim commits the heinous crime of murdering their child it's called an honor killing. When a non-Muslim does it, it's called simply a murder. Honor killings are a cultural problem, prevalent in Sikh, Hindu cultures, as well as some Muslim cultures. There is a difference between a culture and the teachings of the religion. Statistically, if you look at people who murder their children for any reason, it will likely outnumber honor killings. But because of the media exposure of the honor killing is magnified to such a degree, that it seems like it's an everyday thing.

Recently there was an alleged honor killing in Dallas, Texas. I use the word "alleged" because the supposed perpetrator of the crime has never been caught; hence the true reasoning behind the killings is yet to be determined. Two girls were killed in a horrific way, allegedly by their Muslim father. This made front-page news. Ironically, at the same time, a non-Muslim man threw *four* of his children off a bridge in Texas, killing them all. In the same issue of the newspaper, this report was tucked away in the middle of the newspaper.[176]

As I write this book, a new double murder-suicide took place in America. A man named Josh Powell brutally killed his 5 and 7-year old sons, chopping them with a hatchet, and burned the house down, killing himself at the same time.

Another case that took place in the last few days was the case of Thomas Lorde and Latasha Jackson. Thomas Lorde killed

---

[176] http://www.dailymail.co.uk/news/article-1176269/Father-killed-children-look-family-photo-day-hes-executed.html

Latasha Jackson and his daughter from her, before turning the gun on himself.

In both of the above cases, in addition to many that take place almost daily throughout America, we never find out the religion of the criminal. Unless it's a Muslim.

These are just some of the hundreds of homicides that take place each year in the United States. We see jilted boyfriends, divorced husbands, people engaging in extra-marital affairs, all resulting in tragic murders because of jealousy, rage or whatever the reason may be. But we never find out the religion of the perpetrators, because it is irrelevant. A murder is a brutal and callous murder, whoever conducted it, whether Muslim, Christian, Jew or atheist.

But the amazing thing is that when a so-called Muslim murders any family member, it's labeled an honor killing, and Islam, the religion as a whole, is blamed.

This shows the double standard that the media employs when reporting Muslim versus non-Muslim acts of crime.

It doesn't help when so-called academics like Robert Spencer try to "prove" that honor killings are actually sanctioned in Islam by providing vague resources that are mistranslated or intentionally misrepresented.

Here is an example of that:

Robert Spencer presents a text, Reliance of the Traveler, as a reference for Islamic law. He quotes where it says, "retaliation is obligatory against anyone who kills a human being purely intentionally and without right." However, "not subject to retaliation" is "a father or mother (or their fathers or mothers) for killing their offspring, or offspring's offspring."

He "forgets" to mention that the article is not referring to what he might call honor killing. It is referring to murder in general, and the reason given for the father not to be punished with capital punishment, according to other sources, is "out of respect for the fatherhood". Unfortunately, the author of *Umdatus-Saalik*, the original text from which the *Reliance of the Traveler* was translated from, has not explained the reason for the ruling. Needless to say, the opinion is not a commonly accepted ruling amongst Islamic jurists.

The text, *Matn Al-Risala* of *Shaikh Ibn Abi Zayd al-Qayrawani*, a *Maliki* jurist, says the following about a father who murders his son: "The blood money is made more exacting in the case [of] a father who kills his son..."

This clearly shows that there is a punishment for a parent that kills its child. However, why isn't the father executed for the homicide?

The commentary of the text notes why the father is not executed: A father "is not executed because of the respect for fatherhood."

However, there is a condition: "If there is any indication that the father actually did intend to kill the son, then the father is killed for the intentional murder, according to the adopted juristic position." So it would seem that the father *not* suffering capital punishment is in the case of *unintentional* killing. In the case of intentional murder, capital punishment will be implemented.

He also quotes a saying of Prophet Muhammad, which he completely misrepresents. Here's the text:

"The Messenger of Allah (may peace be upon him) used not to kill the children, so thou shouldst not kill them unless you could know what Khadir had known about the child he killed, or you could distinguish between a child who would grow up to be a believer (and a child who would grow up to be a non-believer), so that you killed the (prospective) non-believer and left the (prospective) believer aside."[177]

To understand what this text means, we must refer to a story of Moses and a person named *Khidar* which is mentioned in the Qur'an. God had bestowed *Khidar* with a special insight and knowledge, with which he could see the future. In the story, he comes across a young child, and kills him to the dismay of Moses, who objects to this seemingly barbaric action.

---

[177] Sahih Muslim Book 019, Number 4457

But later on *Khidar* explains to Moses that this child was going to grow up to be rebellious towards his parents, and because of that God had instructed him to kill the child, and God subsequently replaced that child with a pious child.

This story, although Muslims believe it to be a true story, is the story of the "supernatural", and has not been adopted by any Islamic scholar as a source to pass religious rulings. No Islamic scholar has taken this story and used it to justify the killing of one's own child.

Now if we go back to the source that Robert Spencer claims is proof that Islam justifies honor killings, we will understand clearly what it means. What the prophet Muhammad's quote means is that nobody has the authority to kill their child unless he is bestowed with the power of *Khidar*, who had God-bestowed knowledge about the future. And because none of us had that power, nobody is authorized to go and kill their children.

The summary is that Robert Spencer is claiming is that a saying of the Prophet Muhammad means the opposite of what it truly means. It is, without a doubt, academically dishonest and completely disingenuous, not to say highly deficient of scholarly standards.

Female Genital Mutilation

This is another of those issues that is portrayed as being Islamic, when it is a cultural issue prevalent in mainly western, eastern, and north-eastern regions of Africa.

There are a few methods adopted to conduct this act. According to the World Health Organization (WHO), they are:

1. Clitoridectomy: partial or total removal of the clitoris (a small, sensitive and erectile part of the female genitals) and, in very rare cases, only the prepuce (the fold of skin surrounding the clitoris).
2. Excision: partial or total removal of the clitoris and the labia minora, with or without excision of the labia majora.
3. Infibulation: narrowing of the vaginal opening through the creation of a covering seal. The seal is formed by cutting and repositioning the inner, or outer, labia, with or without removal of the clitoris.
4. Other: all other harmful procedures to the female genitalia for non-medical purposes, e.g. pricking, piercing, incising, scraping and cauterizing the genital area.

There are no medical benefits to this practice, and the practice is done, according to its practitioners "to curb the sexual desire" of the woman, or to "prevent her from illicit acts before marriage".

There is actually more harm to the female health through this practice, with things like infections being the most common.

Other complications include:

1. Recurrent bladder and urinary tract infections;
2. Cysts;
3. Infertility;
4. An increased risk of childbirth complications and newborn deaths

   Other complications

The figures given on the WHO website are staggering, with an estimated 92 million girls having undergone a FGM procedure in Africa.

The WHO, in addition to other United Nations agencies has made it an objective to eradicate this practice.

Although some of the practitioners of this barbaric act consider it a religious act, there are no valid religious texts to support it.

Islamophobes have also used this issue to stoke up misunderstandings about Islam. Ayaan Ali Hirsi, who was mentioned earlier, alleges that she was a victim of the practice. Interestingly enough, her father, obviously a Muslim, was against it, but when he was absent her grandmother, following the prevalent culture in Somalia, forced her to have it done.

Without a doubt, in Somalia, where she is from, this is practiced, but in no way does that reflect upon all Muslims throughout the world.

From an Islamic perspective, if we look at the majority of Islamic countries, we find that FGM is not practiced there. Saudi Arabia, supposedly practicing a rigid interpretation of Islam, do not practice it, neither do any of the other Middle Eastern and Gulf countries. It is unheard of in the Indian sub-continent and most Asian countries.

To summarize, Female Genital Mutilation is certainly a problem in many African countries. Muslims should be vocal in condemning this action, and advocate for the eradication of the practice.

Arranged Marriages

Many people think "arranged" is synonymous with "forced". However this is not true. The traditional method of marriage in Islam is that the parents seek a husband or wife for their son and daughter, and if they know a particular family that is suitable for their child, they approach them and ask for their hand in marriage.

There is a lot of wisdom in this approach, the most prominent one being that when someone falls in love, the love for the person clouds their judgment, and they make a decision that they regret later. As the saying goes, "Love is blind". Parents, when choosing a spouse for their child go into the arrangement after evaluating all the pros and cons of the proposal, and make an informed decision, then make a proposal that is suitable for their child.

The final decision is then made by the children themselves. If they refuse to marry the proposed fiancée, the parents cannot force them. It is against the teachings of Islam.

Do some parents go against this rule? Absolutely, they do force their children into marriage, against their will. But this is not permissible according to Islam, and it is a cultural issue prevalent amongst many religions, including Sikhism and Hinduism.

To summarize, arranged marriages are *not* forced marriages. Arranged means arranged by the parents, agreed to by the child.

Dhimmi....what does it mean?

The word *Dhimmi* is one of the favorite words of the people that are critical of Islam. This word is widely portrayed as meaning people who are suffering "subjugation" or "submission" or words similar in nature.

The reality, as is the norm with most of the things that the Islamophobes portray, is very different.

The word *Dhimmi* is derived from the word *Dhimmah,* which means "responsibility, agreement, mutual contract" etc. In fact, another name given to *Dhimmis* is *Mu'aahid,* which means "one who makes an agreement". (See below hadith).

So the actual definition of the word *Dhimmi* is "that non-Muslim who lives in a Muslim-ruled government and by paying his or her taxes becomes the *responsibility* of the Muslim state".

How important is this "responsibility"? We can judge by reading the following sayings of the prophet Muhammad:

"Whoever killed a *Mu'aahid* (a person who is granted the pledge of protection by the Muslims) shall not smell the fragrance of Paradise though its fragrance can be smelt at a distance of forty years (of traveling)."[178]

---

[178] Sahih Al-Bukhari, Volume 9, Book 83, Number 49.

The Messenger of Allah (saw) said: "He who harms a person under covenant, or charged him more than he can, I will argue against him on the Day of Judgment."[179]

The Messenger of Allah (saw) said: "He who hurts a hurts me, and he who hurts me annoys Allah."[180]

In support of the above ahadith (sayings of Prophet Muhammad) a Maliki scholar states:

"The covenant of protection obligates upon us certain responsibilities toward the ahl al-dhimmah. They are our neighbors, under our shelter and protection upon the guarantee of Allah, His Messenger, and the religion of Islam. Whoever violates these obligations against any one of them by so much as an abusive word, by slandering his reputation, or by doing him some injury or assisting in it, has breached the guarantee of Allah, His Messenger (saw), and the religion of Islam."[181]

Thomas Arnold describes the relations between dhimmi and Muslim communities in Spain under Islamic rule.

"The toleration of the Muhammadan government towards its Christian subjects in Spain and the freedom of intercourse between the adherents of the two religions brought about a certain amount of assimilation in the two communities. Inter-marriages became frequent; Isidore of Beja, who fiercely inveighs against the Muslim

---

[179] Narrated by Yahya b. Adam in the book of Al-Kharaa
[180] Tabarani in Al-Awsat, with a good chain
[181] Shaha al-Deen al-Qarafi, Al-furuq

conquerors, records the marriage of 'Abd al-Aziz, the son of Musa, with the widow of King Roderick, without a word of blame. Many of the Christians adopted Arab names, and in outward observances imitated to some extent their Muhammadan neighbors, e.g. many were circumcised, and in matters of food and drink followed the practice of the "unbaptized pagans".[182]

As for the *Jizyah* that was paid by the non-Muslims in Muslim governments, it entitled to them to all the services available in the country, in addition to the full protection and backing of the government, without any prejudice. It is well established in all developed countries that if you want to benefit from the services that the government provides, you must pay your taxes. Living in a Muslim country was no different. To have services provided to the, the population had to pay their fair share of taxes, whether Muslim or non-Muslim.

---

[182] Thomas W. Arnold, 'The Preaching of Islam,' Second Edition, Kitab Bhavan Publishers, New Delhi, p. 128

What we can learn from the Arab Spring

This book would be incomplete without mentioning one of the greatest peaceful revolutions of the 21st century, the Arab Spring.

Dictators have lost seats of power after decades of iron-fisted rule. Some of those dictators were well known to be supported by our government, which turned a blind eye to the dictators' tyranny because of their protection of Israel, also giving them incentives to maintain the status quo by filling their bank accounts with billions in financial aid.

But no government could stop the willpower of the people that demanded change. When the people were desperate for change, they adopted peaceful means of protest and demonstrations, gathering in their thousands, sometimes hundreds of thousands to demand that these decades-old rulers leave; and it worked! Their persistence paid off, and many countries' populations are now hoping for a better future with freedom and liberty after many years of hopelessness and despair.

So what can we learn from this? There are a few points that we must keep in mind:

1. Freedom is something sought after by everyone.

2. If we support governments that are oppressive to their people, with the excuse that "it's in our national interest" to do so, or because the oppressive regimes "are our friends", those people will undoubtedly detest us.

3. Attacking countries with the excuse of removing their dictators and to impose democracy is counter-productive. Change must come from within, and the Arab Spring has shown that when people want freedom and democracy desperately enough, they will get it by themselves, without outside interference.

4. The Arab Spring should also teach a lesson to terrorists, who have only understood violence and killing to attempt change in their society. This revolution clearly sends a message to the extremists that we don't need violence to overthrow corrupt governments, and that the ends, however high and noble they may seem, do not justify the means. There is a peaceful way of doing things, and that is the most effective way.

5. In conflict-ridden areas, discussion and dialogue is extremely important. To have a blanket policy of "not discussing peace with terrorists" leads to stalemates. When Britain sat down with the IRA, (Irish Republican Army) a terrorist organization responsible for many

bombings and murder in Britain, a decades-old conflict was resolved, leading to peace in Northern Ireland.

Ironically, the Arab Spring has been either totally ignored by the Islamophobes, or portrayed as being orchestrated by Islamic fundamentalists. The reason for this is that the Islamophobes don't want to portray Arabs as capable of peaceful change.

The reality is that as the Arab Spring erupted early this year in Tunisia, Egypt and many other states in the Middle East and North Africa, it exposed that not Muslims, but it is actually the dictatorial Arab regimes that are incompatible with democracy. The protests were very much secular in nature as the protesters called for more political freedom, not more religion.

For our governments, it is important to realize that in the past, it was possible to secretly support tyrannical dictators, without any kinds of repercussions. In the past, news about what was going on behind borders of countries was largely invisible to outsiders' eyes, and information took years to get out beyond the borders. But in the age of the Internet, and social media such as Facebook and Twitter, news and information travels through the "information super-highway" in seconds. The tyranny of those regimes is disclosed to the world at large in minutes, and the supporters of those regimes are also exposed, resulting in a bad reputation for such supporting nations.

Once all the above issues become clear, it will become apparent that Western nations need to rethink their strategy in the Middle East and in other Muslim countries, vis-à-vis their diplomacy, national interest, and future outlook.

What have people said about Islam and Prophet Muhammad?

I have collected some notable quotes from people who actually studied the life of the Prophet. Most of the quotes are from non-Muslim authors.

I will end this book with these quotes, and the following request to my non-Muslim friends; please, do your own research about Islam. Read the *Qur'an* yourself, read books on Islam written by objective, fair authors. You will truly find that the myths propagated by the critics of Islam hold no weight against the true reality.

Here are the quotes:

A British historian writes about the attacks made on the Prophet Muhammad in the 19th century:

"Alas, such theories are very lamentable. If we would attain to knowledge of anything in God's true Creation, let us disbelieve them wholly! They are the product of an Age of Skepticism: they indicate the saddest spiritual paralysis, and mere death-life of the souls of men: more godless theory, I think, was never promulgated in this Earth. A false man found a religion? Why, a false man cannot build a brick

house! [...] It will not stand for twelve centuries, to lodge a hundred and eighty millions; it will fall straightway."[183]

Karen Armstrong, in her ground-breaking book, *Muhammad: A Prophet for Our Time*, says:

"We have a long history of Islamophobia in Western culture that dates back to the time of the Crusades. This distorted version of the Prophet's life became one of the received ideas of the West, and Western people have always found it difficult to see Muhammad in a more objective light. Muhammad was not a man of violence. We must approach his life in a balanced way, in order to appreciate his considerable achievements."[184]

"As a paradigmatic personality, Muhammad has important lessons, not only for Muslims, but also for Western people. His life was a jihad: as we shall see, this word does not mean 'holy war,' it means 'struggle.' Muhammad literally sweated with the effort to bring peace to war-torn Arabia, and we need people who are prepared to do this today. His life was a tireless campaign against greed, injustice, and arrogance."[185]

"The young Muhammad was well-liked in Mecca. He was handsome, with a compact, solid body of average height. His hair and beard were

---

[183]"On Heroes, Hero-Worship, and The Heroic in History", May 8th,1840. p- 26

[184] Karen Armstrong: *Muhammad: A Prophet for Our Time,* pages 16-17

[185] Ibid p-19

thick and curly, and he had a strikingly luminous expression and a smile of enormous charm, which is mentioned in all the sources. He was decisive and wholehearted in everything he did, so intent on the task at hand that he never looked over his shoulder, even if his cloak got caught in a thorny bush. When he did turn to speak to somebody, he used to swing his entire body around and address him full face. When he shook hands, he was never the first to withdraw his own."[186]

"Khadijah was impressed and proposed marriage to him. She needed a new husband and her talented kinsman was a suitable choice: "I like you because of our relationship,"she told him, "and your high reputation among your people, your trustworthiness, good character, and truthfulness."

"Some of Muhammad's critics have sneered at this timely match with the wealthy widow, but this was no marriage of convenience. Muhammad loved Khadijah dearly, and even thought polygamy was the norm in Arabia, he never took another, younger, wife while she was alive."[187]

"Khadijah wrapped him in a cloak and held him in her arms until his fear abated. She had no doubts at all about the revelation. This was no jinn, she insisted. God would never play such a cruel trick on a man who had honestly tried to serve Him. 'You are kind and considerate to your kin,' she reminded him. 'You help the poor and forlorn and bear

---

[186] Ibid p-37
[187] Ibid p-38

their burdens. You are striving to restore the high moral qualities that your people have lost. You honor the guest and go to the assistance of those in distress. This cannot be, my dear.'"[188] "The American scholar Michael Sells describes what happens when the driver of a hot, crowded bus in Egypt plays a cassette of Qur'anic recitations:

'A meditative calm begins to set in. People relax. They jockeying for space ends. The voices of those who are talking grow quieter and less strained. Others are silent, lost in thought. A sense of shared community overtakes the discomfort.'"[189]

"A partially personified female figure was central to nearly all the early revelations. We find veiled allusions to a woman conceiving a child or giving birth; the image of a woman who has lost her only child, and the poignant evocation of a baby girl, murdered by her disappointed parents. This strong female presence was remarkable in the aggressive patriarchy of Mecca and may explain why women were among the first to respond to the message of the Qur'an."[190]

"...if they practiced hilm, Muslims would look after the weak and disadvantaged, liberate their slaves, counsel each other to patience and compassion, and feed the destitute, even when they were hungry themselves. Muslims must always behave with consummate gentleness and courtesy. They were men and women of peace: 'For true servants

---

[188] Ibid p-48
[189] Ibid p-59
[190] Ibid p-60

of the Most Gracious are they who walk gently on the earth, and who, whenever the jahilun address them, reply 'Peace'""[191]
"On their way home from Badr, Muhammad uttered an important and oft-quoted maxim: "We are returning from the Lesser Jihad (the battle) and going to the Greater Jihad,"--the immeasurably more important and difficult struggle to reform their own society and their own hearts."[192]

"Constantly the Qur'an insists upon the importance of mercy and forgiveness, even during armed conflict. And although it is important to fight persecution and oppression, the Qur'an constantly reminds Muslims that it is much better to sit down and solve the problem by courteous discussion. True, God permitted retaliation in the Torah-- eye for eye, tooth for tooth--'but he who shall forgo it out of charity will atone better for some of his past sins.'"[193]

"Muhammad was an indulgent husband. He insisted that his wives live frugally in their tiny, sparse huts, but he always helped them with the household chores and looked after his own personal needs, mending and patching his clothes, cobbling his shoes, and rending the tending the family goats."[194]

"In the pre-Islamic period, a woman could not own property. Any wealth that came her way belonged to her family and was administered by her male relatives. [...] The Qur'an bluntly refutes this

---

[191] Ibid p-80
[192] Ibid p-137
[193] Ibid p-136
[194] Ibid p-139

behavior and takes it for granted that a woman has an inalienable right to her inheritance. [...] The Qur'an was attempting to give women a legal status that most Western women would not enjoy until the 19th century. The emancipation of women was a project dear to the Prophet's heart..."[195]

"Later in the Islamic empires, Jews would enjoy full religious liberty..."[196]

"Western critics also persist in viewing the Prophet of Islam as a man of war, and fail to see that from the very first he was opposed to the jahili arrogance and egotism that not only fueled the aggression of his time but is much in evidence in some leaders, Western and Muslim alike, today. The Prophet, whose aim was peace and practical compassion, is becoming a symbol of division and strife--a development that is not only tragic but also dangerous to the stability on which the future of our species depends."[197]

"If we are to avoid catastrophe, the Muslim and Western worlds must learn not merely to tolerate but to appreciate one another. A good place to start is with the figure of Muhammad: a complex man, who resisted facile, ideologically-driven categorization, who sometimes did things that were difficult or impossible for us to accept, but who had profound genius and founded a religion and cultural tradition that

---

[195] Ibid p-146-147
[196] Ibid p-163
[197] Ibid pp212-213

was not based on the sword but whose name--"Islam"--signified peace and reconciliation."[198]

---

[198] Ibid p-214

Acknowledgements and Recommended Reading

1. http://www.publiceye.org/liberty/training/Muslim_Menace_Complete.pdf
2. www.loonwatch.com
3. www.whyislam.com
4. www.islam.thetruecall.com
5. www.adl.org
6. www.cnn.com
7. www.Wikipedia.org
8. www.cwgc.org
9. www.ispu.org
10. The Holy Quran, with footnotes, Abdullah Yusuf Ali
11. www.englishtafseer.com
12. www.theamericanmuslim.com
13. www.thinkprogress.org
14. www.biggovernment.com
15. http://thinkprogress.org/
16. www.pfaw.org
17. www.who.int/en
18. www.newyorktimes.com
19. Karen Armstrong: *Muhammad: A Prophet for Our Time*
20. www.guardian.co.uk
21. www.wnd.org
22. www.bbc.co.uk

23. www.youtube.com

24. www.peshitta.org

25. http://www.sanford.duke.edu

26. www.rand.org

27. www.chrgj.org

28. www.dailymail.co.uk

29. www.familysecuritymatters.org

30. *The Grand Mosque of Paris: A Story of How Muslims Rescued Jews During the Holocaust* by Karen Gray Ruelle.

Index